CONCILIUM
THEOLOGY IN THE AGE OF RENEWAL

CONCILIUM

EXECUTIVE EDITORIAL COMMITTEE

CONCILIUM/VOL. 11

DOGMA

WHO IS JESUS OF NAZARETH?

Volume 11

CONCILIUM
theology in the age of renewal

PAULIST PRESS
NEW YORK, N.Y. / GLEN ROCK, N.J.

PAULIST PRESS
EXECUTIVE OFFICES: 304 W. 58th Street, New York, N.Y. and 21 Harristown Road, Glen Rock, N.J.
Executive Publisher: John A. Carr, C.S.P.
Executive Manager: Alvin A. Illig, C.S.P.
Asst. Executive Manager: Thomas E. Comber, C.S.P.

EDITORIAL OFFICES: 304 W. 58th Street, New York, N.Y.
Editor: Kevin A. Lynch, C.S.P.
Managing Editor: Urban P. Intondi

Printed and bound in the United States of America by
The Colonial Press Inc., Clinton, Mass.

CONTENTS

PART III

DOCUMENTATION CONCILIUM

PREFACE

Edward Schillebeeckx, O.P/*Nijmegen, Netherlands*

Boniface Willems, O.P./*Nijmegen, Netherlands*

For twenty centuries now the unlimited and redemptive presence of God in the man Jesus—that fundamental fact of the Bible and that most original matter of revelation—has been the object of continual reflection. Men of all times approach this mystery with the predetermined images and associations of the spiritual and socio-economic milieu in which they live, and as a result, there are always new and different lights on the unique mystery of Christ. This has been verified in Sacred Scripture itself, where the Judaeo-Christian world and the Hellenistic world regard this mystery from different points of view. The same mystery of Christ arrived at in diverse ways finds wide varieties of expression.

At present, when there is a special partiality for an existential manner of speaking, and consequently, within this framework, for the historical dimension of human existence, we see a change, especially since World War II. A new accent characterizes the contemporary approach to the mystery of Christ when compared to the old manuals of christology.

In this volume we wish to give a general view of the change and to establish, more or less, the present situation in Catholic dogma, without attempting a strictly hermeneutical approach, by studying the Christ of history, the Christ of the Bible, and

1

the Christ of dogma. A selective choice had to be made, of course.

In the first article (Yves Congar), *functional* revelation is examined; God's revelation is accomplished in and through a history of salvation, in which God shows us, by his active intervention among men, who he really is. In the second article (J. Bourke), there is a brief survey of the controversy stirred up by R. Bultmann. All this brings us to the acceptance, with all the consequences entailed, of the fact that Jesus is truly man: *kenosis* as studied by P. Schoonenberg. Lastly, there is the basic problem of resurrection and redemption (J. González Ruiz).

In the articles with a more bibliographical slant, two other christological subjects are treated: the human consciousness of Jesus Christ (E. Gutwenger) and the relation of the glorified Christ to the world (H. Riedlinger and O. Rousseau).

We are aware of not having completely explained in this brief speculative work the "problem of Christ" as it has been formulated in recent years, but we consider that it is only by this "speculative" information that the wide public of CONCILIUM can be introduced in a measure to the problems which have arisen lately with regard to the question: who is Jesus of Nazareth?

PART I

ARTICLES

Yves Congar, O.P./*Strasbourg, France*

Christ in the Economy of Salvation and in Our Dogmatic Tracts

Our age is an age of great theological production, due in large measure to the increasing importance of universities and similar institutions that insist on going beyond a passive repetition of standard theses, and on taking into account what other disciplines, especially those concerned with source materials, may contribute to these theses.

This is particularly true in the study of Sacred Scripture. While a considerable number of Protestant exegetes have rejected the radicalism of their predecessors, Catholic exegesis, profiting by the work of pioneers and by the liberties granted in *Divino afflante* ("that liberating encyclical", as Pius XII liked to refer to it), is approaching the texts with a fresh outlook that is quite a change. It has embraced with wisdom and moderation a method that is thoroughly historical and philological. In so doing, there is bound to be at times an alarming confusion among theologians in possession of a centuries-old heritage. The unfortunate consequence is not that they are upset; it is the resulting divorce that might be established between the research of biblical scholars and the conclusions of theologians. An unhealthy situation of "double truth" might ensue, which must be avoided at all costs. One group must pay close attention to the work of the other in a common fidelity to the tradition of the Church.

5

Unquestionably a firstfruit of this renewed study of the sources has been the realization that Christianity is a history. The revelation contained in the Old and New Testaments is presented neither as a code, nor a catechism, nor a list of propositions, but as a history of what God has done in the lives of men, for humanity as a whole, in order to fulfill in them the design of grace. All this history tends toward one end or term, with reference to which all its stages are explained and find their meaning. Eschatology has enjoyed one of the most decisive revivals of the last half century, not only as the last chapter of a static theology but also as determining the very meaning and direction in which history unfolds. Now all this history also has a center in the fact of Jesus Christ, in whom what we await has already come to us in principle or in germ. That is why our preaching and our catechesis, once more inspired by the liturgy and wedded to this movement, have again become christological and historical, centered on the "Christian mystery" and ultimately on the paschal mystery which is, as it were, the heart of all Christian mystery.

But the problems created for classical theology by exegetes returning to biblical sources must be recognized and faced. For centuries past, especially since the great Scholastics who proposed such a seemingly definitive and perfect elaboration of sacred doctrine, theology has been formulated satisfactorily in ontological terms. Its work was to contemplate and define by means of revelation the *en-soi* of God and of Christ, that is, *what* they are in themselves. And now biblical scholars agree more and more in affirming that revelation comes to us essentially in the framework of history and that it is essentially "economic" or "functional":[1] there is no revelation of the mystery

---

[1] We use certain words in a technical sense: *Ontology* means knowledge of a reality in itself (that which it is) in terms of being. The *Economy* means the historical order of what God has done for our salvation, the realization in history of his Plan of grace. *Functional* (economic, economical) is used in contrast to absolute or *en-soi:* a functional revelation is a revelation conditioned, measured by its relation to our salvation, a revelation by and in the Economy.

of God and Christ except in the testimony handed on about what they did and are doing *for us,* that is, except in relation to our salvation. This will become clear if we look at an example drawn from the Old Testament and then at several christological studies.

If there is a passage in which God seems to define *what* he is in himself, it is certainly Exodus 3, 14: *Ego sum qui sum.* Etienne Gilson continually shows the role that the "metaphysics of Exodus" has played in Christian thought. Thomas Aquinas had good reason to see in this statement a revealed formula corresponding to the highest reach of human reason concerning the nature of God: *Ipsum esse subsistens,* God who IS absolute Act, who IS simply pure act. The principal attributes that can be affirmed of him are here indicated. In fact, the translation of *eyeh asher eyeh* from the Hebrew as "I am he who is," is perfectly valid. It has the support of the Septuagint. This also is the source of the translation of the Name of God, Yahweh, by "The Eternal One", found in French Protestant Bibles. However, today there is agreement upon the fact that an ontological preoccupation was foreign to the Jewish Old Testament. Other translations are possible and, supported by serious considerations, they share the approval of specialists: "I am who I am": God will not give his Name! [2] or, the Hebrew verb in the causative, "I am (I will be) he who makes being." [3]

A fourth translation is possible, more consonant, we believe,

[2] Among Catholic writers, A. Dubarle, "La signification du nom de Jahweh," in *Revue de sciences philosophiques et théologiques* 34 (1951), pp. 3-21, approved by G. Lambert, "Que signifie le nom de YHWH?", in *Nouvelle Revue Théologique* 74 (1952), pp. 897-915; see also C. Cunliffe, "The Divine Name of Yahweh," in *Scripture* 6 (1954), pp. 112-115; M. Allard, "Note sur la formule 'Ehyeh ašer Ehyeh,' " in *Recherches de Science religieuse* 45 (1957), pp. 79-86. There is a history and classification of the interpretations in M. Reisel, *The Mysterious Name of YHWH* (Assens, 1957); R. Mayer, "Der Gottesname Jahwe im Lichte der neuesten Forschung," in *Biblische Zeitschrift* 2 (1958), pp. 35-53.

[3] A. Barrois, *Manuel d'archeologie biblique II* (Paris, 1953), p. 404. E. Dhorme, "Le nom du Dieu d'Israël," in *Revue de l'Histoire des Religions* 141 (January, 1952), pp. 5-18, denies this causative meaning; he accepts the meaning "he exists". Cf. Ludwig H. Koehler, *Old Testament Theology* (Philadelphia, 1957). (The one who is, who lives.)

with the general meaning of the Bible and substantially similar to what is accepted by many biblical scholars. The verb that is translated by "I am" is in the future, exactly as in verse 12, where no one hesitates to translate "I will be with you". One should write therefore: "I will be he who (or what) I will be." [4] But is that an answer? Moses asked: If they ask me your name, what shall I answer them? And God answers: My Name? Who am I? You will see by my acts. I am, I will be the one who will lead you to Sinai, who will give you the Law there, who will make an alliance with you, the one who will make a people of you, his people. I will be the one who nourishes you in the desert, who will make you enter the land that I promised you. I am, I shall be the one who dwells in the Temple, who will speak to you by the prophets; I am, I shall be the one who always come to you . . . In fact, at the end of the biblical revelation, the Apocalypse gives to the Lord, who is going to effect his supreme "unveiling" for this land, the compound title that should be read as if it were a single word: "He is, he was, he is to come" (Apoc. 1, 4. 8; 4, 8; compare 11, 17; 16, 5). This name corresponds to the one in Exodus. Here, as there, God designates himself as the sovereign subject of sacred history, the "nature" of which is revealed in and by what he is and does for us. Apparently the pronouncement of revelation that is most metaphysical, most ontological, refers to the Economy[5] as the place where and by means of which it is to be understood. God is revealed as one who is *there,* constantly *present; near* men, *with* his people: the God of the alliance.

As is well known, St. John's Gospel repeatedly puts on the lips of Jesus declarations that begin with the words "I am": I am the bread of life, I am the light of the world, the good shepherd, the way, the truth and the life, the true vine, etc.[6]

---

[4] This interpretation is that of M. Reisel, *Observations on 'Ehyeh ašer Ehyeh' (Ex. III, 14). H W'H' (D.S.D., VIII, 13) and sm hmpws.* (Athens, 1957) (cf. *Ephemerides Theologicae Lovanienses,* 1958, 553); M. Allard, *loc. cit.,* cf. footnote 2.

[5] See footnote 1.

[6] A study of these texts has been made by E. Schweizer, *Ego eimi . . .*

These affirmations go beyond simple comparisons or parables; they have a definite value in revealing *what* Jesus is. But how? —by designating Christ as the subject (not defined in himself) of soteriological actions relating to the Economy.[7] Most of the images that the verb "I am" introduces are very expressive. They must be given their exact epistemological status. In the Old Testament, God was called the Rock of Israel, or a spring of water. But God *is* neither a mineral nor a liquid. Comparisons are to be taken in accord with the laws of analogy. In this case one is confronted with a particular case of proportional analogy: God, Christ, are for the faithful what a spring or bread is for an exhausted body. But this kind of analogy is called "improper" because it does not apply directly to a similarity in being but merely to a similarity in effects.[8]

God does something for our souls similar to what water and bread do for an exhausted body. This type of statement lends itself consequently to expressing very well not the *en-soi* of God or of Christ, but what they do for us, that is, their economic reality or their functional truth, which of course presupposes a corresponding *en-soi*, as we shall explain later. But if one reflects on the fact that the revelation of God, of Christ, of the Church and of grace has been made for the most part in images, one is led to admit that it is, to that extent, economic.

It is obviously impossible within the limits of this article (and it is not necessary for its objective) to enumerate even the principal themes and christological texts. It will suffice to recognize a tendency with regard to certain texts or themes, confining ourselves to certain works devoid of all extremism.[9]

Die religions-geschichtliche Herkunft und theologische Bedeutung der johanneischen Bildreden . . . (Göttingen, 1939).

[7] Cf. A. Feuillet, *Johannine Studies* (New York: Alba House, 1965).

[8] Cf. M. Penido, *Le rôle de l'analogie en théologie dogmatique Bibliothèque Thomiste* 15 (Paris, 1931), pp. 42f., 99f., 107f.; Y. Congar, *La Foi et la Théologie* (Paris, 1962), pp. 30-3.

[9] We shall mention especially J. Dupont, *Essais sur la Christologie de S. Jean* (Bruges, 1951); L. Cerfaux, *Christ in the Theology of St. Paul* (New York, 1959); E. Boismard, *The Prologue of St. John's Gospel*

Here is a fact not without profound significance: the formulas with the most dogmatic content and emphasis are often found in doxologies: the Church confesses the plenitude of its faith in the praises offered in its worship.[10] If one rereads, for instance, the christological hymn of Philippians 2, 6-11, one is struck first of all by the fact that, here as elsewhere, St. Paul does not distinguish in Christ what stems from the divine nature and what from the human nature. He speaks simply of Christ and attributes to him both the preexistence of divinity and the annihilation of the cross. As to what concerns preexistence, he goes into no metaphysical precision about life within the Godhead: the idea and the term *morphē* (the form or condition of existence) are of course part of our dogma of the incarnation, but for St. Paul they are also related to salvation history. The only theological pronouncements or revelations about the *en-soi* of God are within the framework of the Economy.

St. John, on the other hand, gives a precise name to the christological preexistent: it is the *Logos*. But Dom J. Dupont notes: "When St. John says that Jesus is not only the bearer of the Word of God, but is that Word itself, his intention is not to define the transcendent nature of the Son of God or to determine the mode of his origin in the Godhead. The term *Logos* does not designate Christ as a proper name or a personal name: it is in his relation to the world and to men that Jesus is found to be the Word of God." [11] E. M. Boismard tries to emphasize the possibilities that these texts bring to speculative theology (in the direction that we ourselves shall point out below), while still holding to the opinions of Dom Dupont with regard to these texts.[12] According to O. Cullmann, the New Testament does not express the idea of the unity of essence or of nature between God and

---

(London, 1957); O. Cullmann, *The Christology of the New Testament* (Philadelphia, 1959).

[10] A remark made famous by Y. Tremel. "Remarques sur l'expression de la foi trinitaire dans l'Eglise apostolique," in *Lumière et Vie* 29 (1956), pp. 41-66.

[11] *Op. cit.*, p. 58. Cf. E. Tobac, "La notion du Christ-Logos dans la littérature johannique," *R.Eh.* 25 (1929), pp. 213-38.

[12] *Op. cit.*, pp. 110, 122-3.

Christ in the titles *Word* and *Son of God*, but merely a unity of operation in the work of revelation.[13] St. John speaks of *Logos* in order to say that the Word was made flesh, that all things were made by him; in short, he speaks of the creative and revealing activity of God or of his existence *for us.*

R. Schnackenburg remarks that a formula such as "the Father is greater than I" (John 14, 28) is difficult to explain in an ontological perspective referring to the nature of things, and that it has to be understood in the perspective of salvation history, which is that of the New Testament.[14] The same is true of an apparently metaphysical pronouncement such as: "I and the Father are one" (John 10, 30), which aims at the unity of operation, not only according to J. Hessen, who is inclined to minimize anything in the way of a speculative and philosophical assertion,[15] but even in the judgment of E. M. Boismard, who is inclined in the opposite direction.[16] Boismard shows likewise that in St. John, the Word is referred to as Life inasmuch as it dispenses life to others: here he differs little from Dom Dupont, who writes: "In saying that the Father has life in himself and that he gave to the Son the power to have life in himself also, Jesus is not making a revelation about the intra-trinitarian relations, nor about the origin of the Son with relation to the Father." [17]

Whenever the title "Son of God" is attributed to Jesus, we can be quite sure, first of all, that it expresses the full affirmation of the divinity of Christ abundantly attested to in the apostolic writings. However, this calls for various comments. First, in St. Paul, with whom it carried a great richness of meaning, Son is not used in isolation as a proper noun or as an absolute defini-

[13] *Op. cit.,* pp. 214, 224, 230f.
[14] R. Schnackenburg, "Zur dogmatischen Auswertung des N.T.," *Exegese und Dogmatik.* Ed. H. Vorgrimler (Mainz, 1962), pp. 122-3.
[15] *Griechische oder biblische Theologie? Das Problem der Hellenisierung des Christentums in neuer Beleuchtung* (Leipzig, 1956), p. 152; he links John 14, 8 with 2 Corinthians 5, 19 and Colossians 2, 9.
[16] *Op. cit.,* p. 20 with note 2.
[17] *Op. cit.,* p. 196; Boismard, *op. cit.,* pp. 30-2.

tion of the being of Christ; it is always modified by a determining element that puts the Son in relation to God or the
world.[18] Second, the apostles liked to refer to Psalm 2, 7: "You
are my Son, this day I have begotten you." The dogmatic theologian will have no difficulty in bringing this statement within
the framework of the dogma of the incarnation, even the dogma
of the Trinity. In the New Testament, however, this verse has
reference to the resurrection. It is because, under the title Son
of God, they are not referring to purely ontological considerations. Divinity involves the enjoyment of a divine condition:
Christ is truly established as Son of God *when* he is raised above
the angels, glorified, assimilated to the lordship of God; in a
word, after accomplishing his descent to us for our salvation.[19] This is an "economic" christology. It has been noted, moreover, that in the gospels Jesus is only called Son during his
public life.[20] Third, it is true that St. John calls him *Monogenous*,
that is, "only-begotten" (John 1, 14), but, in a context that is
significant, he adds "of the Father", which suggests the temporal
mission of the Son, as is clearly the case in other passages also

[18] Cf. L. Cerfaux, *op. cit.*, p. 449: "These connections are not limited
to the transcendental relationships of the Father and Son, but are those
of God and of Christ, and embody Christ in his work upon the world
and Christians. In the words in Colossians 1, 15, *prōtotokos pasēs ktiseōs*,
the adjective describes the qualities of the Son in relation to God the
creator: we could say that the adjective has one eye on the transcendence
and the other on the creation."

[19] Cf. Acts 13, 33; Heb. 1, 5; 5, 5; cf. Rom. 1, 4 and the theophany
at the baptism of Jesus: Matt. 3, 17; Mark 1, 11; Luke 3, 22. See J. Dupont, " 'Filius meus es tu,' the interpretation of Ps. 11, 7 in the N.T.,"
in *Recherches de Science religieuse* 35 (1948), pp. 522-43; P. Michalon,
"L'Eglise corps mystique du Christ glorieux," in *Nouvelle Revue Théologique* (July, 1952), pp. 673-87; M. Boismard, "Constitué Fils de Dieu
(Rom. 1, 4)," in *Revue Biblique* 60 (1953), pp. 5-17.

[20] Cf. A. Dubarle, "Les fondements bibliques du Filioque," in *Russie
et Chrétienté* (1950), pp. 229-44, esp. p. 232. He mentions that the
earliest Fathers of the Church confined themselves to the biblical usage
and made a certain distinction between the Son (a title associated with
revelation *ad extra*) and the *Logos;* for example, Tertullian: cf.
A. D'Alès, *La théologie de Tertullien* (Paris, 1905), p. 95; and Hyp-
polytus: cf. B. Capelle, "Le Logos Fils de Dieu dans la théologie d'Hyp-
polyte," in *Recherches de Théologie Ancienne et Médiévale* (1937),
pp. 109-24.

where St. John uses the same expression.[21] Obviously it cannot be stripped of its "theological" implications; neither should it be removed from its "economical" context.

In fact the whole revelation of the Blessed Trinity is economic, since the divine persons are presented in their relation to redeemed man and the work of Christ the redeemer.[22] This is to be expected, as we shall see, because of the very nature of revelation: it is a revealing of salvation, and completely ordered to salvation. When setting out to study the christology of St. Paul, L. Cerfaux begins with soteriology. In so doing he follows closely in the steps of St. Paul, according to the chronology of the epistles, where he proceeds from the resurrection that established Jesus as Lord and ends by emphatically affirming the pre-existence of Christ as God in his cosmic role.[23]

Since we have inherited the conceptualism not of the great Scholastics but of the manuals of Scholastic philosophy, and necessarily opposed as we are to the religious subjectivism of liberal Protestantism and modernism, we often act as if revela-

[21] John 3, 15-17; 1 John 4, 9. Cf. the remarks of Boismard, Le Prologue, 73 (footnote 7). O. Cullmann for his part notes, "The New Testament does not describe for us the being of him who is 'in the bosom of the Father' by an explanation of his nature, but by the initiation of the Son in the integral knowledge of the Father in view of his plan of salvation. That is, he affirms the divine being and the divine personality of the Word without explaining them other than as the utterly unique divine function *in which they manifest themselves* and he affirms that titles such as 'Word', 'Lord' (*Kyrios*), etc., express this. This proves that the New Testament, *even while presupposing the divine being and the divine person of Christ, preexisting,* does not envisage them from the angle of their origin and nature, but from the point of view of their manifestation in the history of salvation." (Reply to Canon G. Bavand, *Choisir* [Geneva], nos. 9-10 [July-August, 1960], p. 21, col. b.) However, one can point out with L. Cerfaux (*op. cit.*, p. 386) that the idea of the Image of God in St. Paul is more "philosophical".

[22] D. Barsotti brings this out in *Vie Mystique et Mystère liturgique* (Paris, 1954), pp. 273f.; H. Rahner, *Theologie de Verkündigung* (Freiburg, 1939), p. 56; they see in the trinitarian mystery as it is revealed in the New Testament the "Vorbegriff der Lehre vom Erlöser".

[23] *Op. cit.*, as a whole and pp. 392f., 399f. This was the train of thought worked out in the minds of the disciples; it had been wrought in the frame of salvation history with regard to the personal quality of Christ. See for example L. Legrand, "L'arrière-plan néo-testamentaire de Lc 1, 35," in *Revue Biblique* 1963, pp. 161-92.

tion were a series of metaphysical propositions, taught us by the divine master and which he alone could teach. Today without sacrificing the objectivity of true teaching with a precise intellectual content, everything inclines us to focus on another, equally important aspect. Yes, everything: mainly, the return to biblical sources that characterizes contemporary theology; the return to the conception of faith as a complete openness toward God which allows him to rule over our lives; the recognition of the Reformation as a radical criticism of a "naive realism" (*chosisme*)[23a] practiced in the later Middle Ages, and an awareness of the personal, dramatic and paradoxical relationship between *my* salvation (created by the beneficent act of God which is Jesus Christ) and myself the sinner in whom the faith, wrought in me by God, has effected this salvation.[24] The Reformation saw Christianity as this relationship continually created by God as Act and Event. Hence its "anti-substantialism", which is a rejection of the static, the general, the ontological in a "chosist" form. The spirit of present-day philosophy also tends in this direction. It no longer aspires after the manner of ancient philosophy to an interpretation of the world as a whole in ontological terms but it gives a reflection of human existence. Consequently, it has opened or reopened the promising subject of interpersonal relations (*i.e.*, "inter-subjective ontology", which is quite different from subjectivism). This helps to create a climate where, in harmony with what biblical research presents, theologians are developing today an interpersonal aspect with respect to religious faith awakened by the Word of God.

[23a] *Chosisme*—"naive realism": Among phenomenologists, *chose* (literally, *thing*) is the correlative of thought. Jean-Paul Sartre says: "By the very act which gives a thing its name, idea becomes thing and makes its entry into the domain of the objective mind." Cf. *L'homme et les choses* (Seglier, 1947). (*Trans.*)

[24] Concerning the opposition between Protestantism and Catholicism, between "personal" and "ontic", cf. J. Hessen, *Platonismus und Prophetismus* . . . (Munich, 1939), pp. 178f.; U. Mann, "Ethisches und Ontologisches in Luthers Theologie," in *Kerygma und Dogma* 3 (1957), pp. 171-207; T. Sartory, *Die ökumenische Bewegung und die Einheit der Kirche* (Meitingen, 1955), pp. 194f.; Y. Congar, *La Tradition et les traditions* I: *Essai historique* (Paris, 1961), p. 78.

There is much to be gained from modern reflections on human existence and interpersonal "I-Thou" relationships with regard to a theology of faith and religious relationships.

The most recent Catholic writings on revelation take all these elements into account although they have not yet said the last word on the subject.[25] Chapter I of the Council's *De Revelatione* presents revelation as the initiative that God takes in the "dialogue of salvation". Pope Paul VI also speaks of this in *Ecclesiam Suam*.[26] As for the new appreciation of faith in the sense of total engagement in obedience to the living God, this is the very heart of present-day renewal in preaching and catechetics. Occupied as we have been by the ecclesiological renewal, we do not give enough attention to this other renewal which is just as important as ecclesiology and has, besides, profound repercussions upon it. But all this calls for a reexamination of revelation and the faith that corresponds to it. By what criteria does a thing fall under the category of revelation? This question is one that would be stated in Scholastic terminology as: what is the formal *quod* of revelation (and of faith)?

St. Thomas did not ask the question in these terms but he approaches it when explaining the "articles" of faith. Certain truths, he says,[27] are revealed, and consequently are objects of faith, *primo et per se,* immediately and by reason of their content, and others are such *secundario, in ordine ad alia,* by concomitance, by their connection with the preceding. But what makes a truth belong to the first category is the relation it has to our supernatural end: such is *per se* an object of faith and

---

[25] Cf. W. Bulst, *Offenbarung. Biblischer und theologischer Begriff* (Düsseldorf, 1960); R. Latourelle, *Théologie de la Révélation. Studia 15* (Paris: Desclée, 1963); R. Schnackenburg, "Zum Offenbarungsgedanken in der Bibel," Biblische Zeitschrift 7 (1963), pp. 2-23 (confrontation with Bultmann.)

[26] *Acta Apostolicae Sedis* 56 (1964), pp. 641f.: "colloquium salutis".

[27] St. Thomas, *II Sent.,* 12, q.1, a.2; *III Sent.,* 24, q.1, a.1, q1. 1 et ad 2; q1. 2 ad 3; *De Veritate,* q. 14, a.8; I-II, q. 106, a.4, ad 2; II-II, q.1, a.6, ad 1; a.8 sol.; q.2, aa. 5, 7; *In Tit.,* c. 3, lect. 2; *Comp. Theol.,* c.2 et 185; cf. *III Sent.,* 24, a. 3, q1. 1 ad 3; I, q. 1, a. 1 (La Révélation—le renseignement sur la fin dernière de l'homme). (Revelation = the teaching of the last end of man.)

therefore of revelation (*id per quod homo beatus efficitur*). In other words he refers to all that is taught concerning what God wants to be and do in view of our salvation and our completion in him, that is, the truth of the perfect religious relationship "quorum visione perfruemur in vita aeterna et per quae ducimur ad vitam aeternam" (whose vision we shall enjoy in eternal life and by which we shall be led to eternal life). The content of revelation is the truth of this religious relationship. Concerning *what* God is, *what* man and the world are, the Word of God has not given us, is not supposed to give us a physical, "ontic" reality: it tells us only what is necessary to insure the truth of the religious and salutary relationship that must unite them all. The complete exposition of the *en-soi* of God (and also of man and the world that science is trying to achieve here below) is reserved for the final vision. In the revelation made to the People of God in its condition as *viator*, we are told about this *en-soi* only what is necessary to secure truth *pour nous*. Revelation is economic (see footnote 1).

However, this much can be said. Neither revelation, nor even kerygma, which is the announcement of salvation, is purely and simply *what* without any *that which*, as extreme Bultmannism would have it.[28] In the economic revelation there are statements about *what* God is and *what* Christ is: these are necessary in order that the religious relationship of faith and salvation may truly exist. Scripture does not know or go beyond the distinction between the *pour-nous* and the *en-soi*, although certain of its functional pronouncements overflow into ontology. A contemporary Jewish biblical scholar, Abraham Heschel, wrote a very profound sentence: "The Bible is not a theology for man, it is an anthropology for God." That is true: the Bible reveals for us the truth of our situation and the covenant we are to establish with God. But it does this really by being first of all, and for that reason, a theology for man. We shall not list here the many

---

[28] This is equivalent to the formula of A. Mallet, "Le problème des concepts et du langage," in *Foi et Vie* (March-April, 1959), pp. 25-37; *idem*, "L'avenir de l'interprétation scripturaire," in *Foi et Vie* (January-February, 1960), pp. 22-43.

pages of our theology, the scriptural pronouncements which concern the *en-soi* of God and Christ.[29] We shall merely show that the development of what economic revelation includes by way of ontological demonstrations is legitimate and necessary.

It was, in effect, normal, at any rate, inevitable, that "the faith once for all given to the saints" (Jude 3) should be formulated more explicitly. This was to be done in two ways, both called forth by the very existence and mission of the Church. On the one hand there was the reflection of the most exacting minds, in conjunction with their human culture and in pursuit of a unity in the domain of the true; on the other, a defense and demonstration of the belief handed down by the apostles against the interpretations and formulations which endangered its meaning and content.[30]

It was normal—because it is the law of the mind as God made it and because he calls upon it to give a response to faith—that people should interpret these as equivalent to scriptural statements. One cannot avoid questions about "being" because one cannot avoid thinking *what* are the realities concerning which the Word of God has made certain pronouncements.[31] We can already identify a first phase of interpretation and investigation of the bare facts and sayings in primitive evangelical history accomplished by the first generation of disciples. These have been incorporated in the later writings of the New Testament itself, especially those of John the theologian.[32] However, the

[29] Interesting suggestions are found in L. Malevez, "Nouveau Testament et théologie fonctionelle," in *Recherches des Sciences Religieuses* 48 (1960), pp. 258-90, esp. p. 279.

[30] See my article, "Théologie," in *Dictionnaire de Théologie catholique,* XV, cols. 346f.; A. Grillmeier, "Vom Symbolum zur Summa," in *Kirche und Ueberlieferung,* edited by J. Betz and H. Fries (Freiburg, 1960), pp. 119-69. French translation: "Du Symbolum à la Summa," in *Eglise et Tradition* (Le Puy/Lyon, 1963), pp. 105-56.

[31] Paul Tillich recalled this need for the use of his Protestant colleagues: *Biblical Religion and the Search for Ultimate Reality* (University of Chicago Press, 1955).

[32] See F. Messner: "Der historische Jesus und der Christus des Glaubens," in *Biblische Zeitschrift* 1 (1957), pp. 224-52; B. Rigaux, "L'historicité de Jésus devant l'exégèse récente," in *Revue Biblique* 65 (1958), pp. 481-522; R. Schnackenburg, "Jesusforschung und Christusglaube," in *Catholica* 13 (1959), pp. 1-17; A. Grillmeier, cf. footnote 30.

second or third generation of disciples tried to think out the christological and trinitarian mystery by making use of these economic formulas of Scripture which were insufficiently developed on the ontological level. This of course led to unsatisfactory expression of the affirmations of "being" enveloped or involved in these formulas. St. Justin, for instance, speaks of the generation of the Word as affirmed in Scripture—how otherwise would one have dared to transfer the idea of generation to God? He seems to identify generation with the act by which God emits a Word *in order to create*.[33] Tertullian sees in the Son and the Spirit the *gradus* of one single substance corresponding to the creative and salvific will of God and to the dynamic unfolding of the divine plan.[34] Origen, formulating his theology of the Trinity as *stemming* from the economic missions, arrives at an idea of the mystery of the Trinity on a subordinate level.[35] The anti-Nicaean theology of the Trinity, so well known, caused *great* difficulties to Petau.

It is very true that the use of philosophical concepts, especially the Platonic, Stoic and Philonian ideas, caused these deviations and brought great minds to conceive of the *Logos* as an intermediary between the transcendent Father and creation or revelation:[36] the Fathers are always denouncing the immoderate use of philosophy as the root of the great heresies.[37]

[33] Cf. G. Aeby, *Les Missions divines de S. Justin à Origène* (Fribourg, 1958), p. 14.

[34] Cf. K. Wölfi, *Das Heilswirken Gottes durch den Sohn nach Tertullian. Anal. Greg. 112* (Rome, 1960); W. Bender, "Die Lehre über den Hl. Geist bei Tertullian," *Münchener Theologische Studien* (S.A.) 18 (Munich, 1961).

[35] Cf. A. Grillmeier, *op. cit.*, footnote 28; French translation pp. 113f.

[36] See R. Arnou, "Platonisme des Pères," in *Dictionnaire de Théologie catholique* XII, cols. 2307, 2319-2320 and especially 2322.

[37] Eusebius remarks on this, *Histoire de l'Eglise*, V, 28, 13. See besides Arnou, *loc. cit.*, J. De Ghellinck, "Un aspect de l'opposition entre Hellénisme et Christianisme. L'attitude vis-à-vis de la dialectique dans les débats trinitaires," in *Patristique et Moyen Age* III (Bruzelles/Paris, 1948), pp. 245-310; G. Bardy, " 'Philosophie' and 'Philosophe' dans le vocabulaire chrétien des premiers siècles," in *Rev. Ascet. et Myst.* 25 (1949), pp. 97-108; P. Hadot, "La Philosophie comme hérésie trinitaire," in *Revue d'Histoire et de Philosophie religieuses* 37 (1957), 236-51.

Now there is involved here the truth of the essential affirmation of the divinity of Christ, which is not only affirmed or presupposed in the formal assertions of Scripture, but required by the overall truth of the work that he accomplished for our benefit (Economy). To save this truth against the Gnostics, St. Irenaeus made the double affirmation that inspires his theology concerning our true union with God. This is founded on the full truth of the divinity of Christ, guaranteed by the authenticity of the apostolic succession with regard to doctrine and ministry. Here, too, are at stake the sovereignty and liberty of God, which could not really be preserved by a *Logos* who (in order to exist as such) had to act as a demiurge of creation and a mediator of revelation.

In order to save the truth of the Economy itself, it was not of course necessary to appeal to a particular philosophy: a St. Athanasius could avoid it by confining himself to a commentary on scriptural texts.[38] However, the status of the realities at stake had to be precisely established as a theology of the *en-soi* of God. One could not stop short at the salutary operations and the functional pronouncements of the Economy: that would have been to risk modalism. Here and there O. Cullmann has undoubtedly given formulas of a modalist tinge,[39] although he is not a modalist in his personal convictions.[40] Even he often sums up the Johannine theology of the Word in these two linked statements: the *Logos* is God, the *Logos* is with God;[41] identity and distinction. But how can one harmonize them in thought, if one does not wish to stop at the threshold of mystery but wishes

[38] See L. Bouyer, "Omoousios. Sa Signification historique dans le symbole de foi," in *Revue de sciences philosophiques et théologiques* (1941), 52-62; Arnou, *op. cit.* (footnote 34), cols. 2259, 2297, 2299, 2343.

[39] We read in *Christologie,* p. 231: "The Logos is God who reveals Himself, who communicates Himself in His action"; on p. 285: "Jesus Christ is God inasmuch as He reveals Himself." P. Gaechter, *Zeitschrift für katholische Theologie* (1960), pp. 88f., brought out this danger in Cullmann, and L. Malevez (*op. cit.,* footnote 27; cf. p. 26 and notes on pp. 267-8) shows clearly the inadequacy of Cullmann's formulas.

[40] Cf. *Christologie,* pp. 214, 286 and *Réponse* (footnote 19).

[41] Cf. *Christologie,* pp. 230f., 270, 286, etc.

to take it in with one's human intelligence, unless one develops a kind of theology of the *en-soi* of the revealed God?

These questions and difficulties of trinitarian theology have their repercussions in christology. Economic revelation would indicate a unity of activities between Christ as "Son" and God the Father, between Jesus and the Son of God he claimed to be. In order to harmonize this essential data and secure the necessary precision, correct thinking about unity and distinction is required. Nestorius was satisfied with a vague union of activities similar to that which Porphyry recognized among incorporeal beings.[42] It was impossible to think out properly the economic assertions concerning Christ's saving action unless the reflection went as far as the level of the *en-soi*. The last manifestations of the insufficiency of strictly functional formulations of this matter were to appear in the 6th century with monothelitism.

In the great trinitarian and christological disputes of the 4th and 5th centuries, the Fathers of the Church made one well-known and correct affirmation concerning the *en-soi* of God, namely, the truth of the Economy taken as a whole. It is well summed up in this frequently repeated formula or in similar terms: He became what we are so as to make us what he is:[43] a formula which in the course of the christological disputes was completed by that other more technical one which unites Economy and ontology: that which is not assumed is not saved. . . .[44] God left his *en-soi* without leaving it in the same way that he entered our world and our history (Economy) in order to make us participators in *his* life, *his* joy, *his* immortality, *his* glory. But this economic view, the commitment, the manifestation and the functional operations that it supposes, require, in order to be true, the full truth of the *en-soi* of Christ and of God, insofar as

[42] Cf. R. Arnou, "Nestorianisme et Néoplatonisme. L'unité du Christ et l'union des 'intelligibles' " in *Gregorianum* 17 (1936), pp. 115-31.

[43] References may be found in our article: "Le moment 'économique' et le moment 'ontologique' dans la Sacra Doctrina," *Mélanges M.-D. Chenu* (1965), p. 83.

[44] *Ibid.*, note 84. And see E. Mersch, *Le corps mystique du Christ. Etude de théologie historique,* Table "Argument sotériologique."

we can speak of this as a result of revelation. St. Athanasius, St. Hilary, St. Cyril of Alexandria never stop arguing from the "economy" to the truth of "theology": if Christ is not true God and true man, we are not divinized . . . Christ only does what he does for us if he *is* what he is in himself. It is because Christ is God that his humanity is redemptive and sanctifying.

From what has just preceded there emerges the truth that revelation is economical and historical. God has made himself known by what he did *for us,* but in this way something of what he is in himself is made known. It is legitimate and normal that the believer should elaborate on these precious elements of knowledge by reflection. We shall conclude this too rapid mention of great problems by suggesting five interesting points that need to be worked on as a consequence of what has been said.

1. Less of the spectacular and more work that issues in learned research and publication are needed to restore the full biblical notion of faith, along with the traditional notion of the Church: one of the two poles of the current renovation. This supposes an effort that would go as far as a new and profound reflection concerning the notion of revelation.

2. Along with this it will be necessary to restore the unity of faith and revelation. Faith does not consist any longer in accepting without proof a long series of propositions any more than revelation consists of just such a list. One of the misfortunes of theology, which spread to preaching and catechetics, was the atomization into articles without an inner union with a living center.[45] On the other hand, Vatican Council I gave to an authentic theology its bill of rights when it proclaimed that faith procures with the grace of God a very fruitful understanding of mysteries by considering the relationships among them and with

[45] This is the situation in theology that Lamennais in 1829 described and deplored in these terms: "Theology, so beautiful in itself, so attractive, so vast, is today, as taught in most seminaries, merely a dried-up and decadent Scholasticism whose dryness repels the students, giving them no overall picture of religion nor its marvelous relevance to all that interests man, in all that can be the object of his thought. It was not conceived in this way by St. Thomas." Quoted by E. Sevrin, *Dom Guéranger et Lamennais* (Paris, 1933), pp. 243-44.

the last end of man.[46] This link we recognize better today as it is manifested by the whole of salvation economy. There is no need to discover it: God himself gave his revelation the unity of his Plan, and this is none other than the salvation and happiness of man (not separated from the universe) by communion with him in Jesus Christ.[47] Is that not what St. Paul called "the mystery"?[48] Is this not what our preaching has rediscovered under the name of "Christian mystery", which also gives its title to various theological undertakings today?[49]

3. One of the results of this rediscovery of unity is that there is no "theology for man" without an "anthropology for God". The greatest misfortune perhaps that has afflicted modern Catholicism is to have concerned itself with theory and catechesis about the *en-soi* of God and religion, without adding to this at all times the significance that this has *for man*. Men and the world without God that we are now living in were born in part as a reaction against such a God without man or the world. The answer to the difficulties that stop many of our contemporaries on the path of faith, and to the challenge of atheism, requires among other things that we always bring out the human impact of the things of God. This by no means means substituting, for a pure presentation of the *en-soi*, a purely humanistic program or an anthropocentric message, which would be to commit the same separatist error as before, only inversely. This *does* mean

[46] *Const. dogm. "Dei Filius,"* c. 4. (Denz. 1796; Denz. Schönmetzer 3016).

[47] A. Möhler defined the essence of Christianity as "the great work which reconciles man with God, the principles guiding the relations of the faithful to Jesus Christ" (*Symbolique,* par. XXXVII).

[48] Cf. Eph. 3, 3f.; Col. 1, 26-27; 2, 2; 4, 3; Rom. 16, 25f.; D. Deden, "Le 'Mystère' paulinien," *Ephemerides Theologicae Lovanienses* 13 (1956), pp. 405-42; M.-J. Le Guillou, *Le Christ et L'Eglise, Théologie du Mystère* (Paris, 1963).

[49] See the whole collection of fascicules under this general title published by Desclée et Cie., 1962; *Mysterium salutis,* published under the direction of Fr. Feirer by Benziger, 1965. His Holiness Paul VI spoke of the foundation in Jerusalem of an Institute devoted to the theology of salvation. For catechetics a profitable book is Fr. Arnold's *Dienst am Glauben* (Freiburg, 1948). French translation: *Serviteurs de la Foi* (Paris, 1957).

that one speaks of the mysteries of God in such a way as to unite a profound perception of what they are in themselves with a vital explanation of what they are *for us:* uniting anthropology for God to theology for man. That is the very genius of revelation, which is economic, in a unique way by its crowning point in Jesus Christ: for in him, the wisdom of God was made man!

4. Sooner or later, speculative theology, drawing upon revelation attested to in Scripture, will have to pose the problem which preoccupies us in a much more personal way: If there is such a deep bond between theology and economy, if God discloses the *en-soi* of his mystery in the *pour-nous* of the covenant of grace and the incarnation, all that has been and is done for us, including the incarnation, has been required, has it not, in spite of his absolute liberty, by what God is *in himself?* Is there not in the mystery of his *en-soi,* a presence, a call for the *pour-nous,* including hominization? The way in which St. Thomas establishes all the activity *ad extra* of nature and grace on the inner generosity of the divinity, stemming from the Father, the principle without principle[50]—a word so pregnant as that of Jesus in St. John 14, 9: "Philip, he who sees me sees also the Father" [51] —the way in which O. Cullmann explains the biblical idea of "Son of Man" with what it seems to imply in the way of a certain eternal existence of the humanity of God:[52] these are so many elements to give food for sober, religious thought, free of all anthroposophic speculation. But we can only state the question here, without even being sure of having explained ourselves properly, having done it so briefly.

5. A certain number of consequences must be envisaged in working out and teaching this theology, consequences which would have repercussions in preaching and catechetics. If a

[50] Cf. our study quoted above, footnote 41: notes 131-135; M. Seckler, *Das Heil in der Geschichte. Geschichtstheologisches Denken bei Thomas v. Aquin* (Munich, 1964).

[51] See "Dum visibiliter Deum cognoscimus," *Les Voies du Dieu vivant* (Paris, 1962), pp. 79-107. German translation in *Wege des lebendigen Gottes* (Freiburg, 1964), pp. 65-98.

[52] See the very stimulating pages in O. Cullmann, *Christologie,* pp. 118-63, with references to the studies of T. Preiss and J. Hering.

renewal is to take place, we think that it would not be by presenting a simple account with commentary of the history of salvation instead of the exposition of a logically worked out synthesis: we have seen that the revealed facts give us the *en-soi* as well as the *pour-nous,* the "theology for man" along with the "anthropology for God" or, to borrow the expressions of Karl Rahner,[53] the essential with the existential. But clearly the economic import of revelation will have to be presented better than it has been done oftentimes. Here are some suggestions.

Let exegetes and theologians take care to know one another by reading and by meetings. We should wish that no canonical grade be conferred in the Church unless the beneficiary has completed and published a work bearing on a biblical question. A need is felt more and more for introducing questions of speculative theology into studies of fact—even of bringing in the dimension of speculative theology deliberately by showing how the questions came up in history with reference to facts. Lastly, it seems necessary to take up again, along with the excellent contributions of Scripture studies today, the tradition, still honored by St. Thomas, of studying the Old Testament and its role as a part of salvation history. This would be to take on a large part of that "concrete historical theology" which His Holiness Paul VI referred to in his allocution to the Observers, on October 17, 1963.

It does not seem to us that an entirely christological theology should be aimed at, such as Karl Barth proposed, nor should the program of E. Mersch be followed with its idea of Christ as the "prime intelligible".[54] Of course we reach a knowledge of the intimate mystery of God only *through* Jesus Christ (*ordo*

---

[53] Article "Dogmatik," in *Lexikon für Theologie und Kirche* III (Freiburg, ²1957), p. 450.

[54] Articles in *Nouvelle Revue Théologique* 61 (1934), pp. 449-75; "Le Christ mystique, centre de la théologie comme science", and in *Recherches de Science religieuse* 26 (1936), 129-57: "L'objet de la théologie et le 'Christus Totus' ", reprinted in abridged form in *La Théologie du Corps mystique* I (Paris, 1944), pp. 56-115.

inventionis, acquisitionis) and from God (*revelationis*),[55] but it is only by means of the mystery of God that we can believe fully in the mystery of the incarnation, and therefore, can understand Jesus Christ (*ordo judicii*). Dogmatic theology must be firmly rooted in the very structure of reality, since after all it is an attempt to reconstruct the great architecture of divine wisdom, a sort of sublime *Poétique* in the sense of Claudel. Then, too, if Christ is the center, the end is none other than God himself (compare 1 Cor. 15, 28). We shall attain through Christ, just as we have known through Christ, that final goal, God and our divinization. That is why, even if there is need for shedding light on ethics and the theology of grace by christology in a way better than St. Thomas did in the *Summa,* there is still no reason to introduce them into christology as a chapter in that study.[56] As for christology, it must take upon itself, as St. Thomas did, but with the resources that excellent biblical and liturgical studies provide, not only the cosmological vision of the Epistles of the Captivity (Teilhard de Chardin), but also a theology of the mysteries of the life and Pasch of Christ, center of the whole Economy.

[55] We admit with Fr. G. Martelet that St. Thomas did not do this sufficiently: "Theologie und Heilsökonomie in der Christologie der 'Tertia Pars' ", in *Gott in Welt, Festgabe K. Rahner* II (Freiburg, 1964), pp. 3-42, esp. pp. 28-42.

[56] Cf. L. Gillon, "L'imitation du Christ et la morale de S. Thomas," in *Angelicum* 36 (1959), pp. 263-286.

Joseph Bourke, O. P./*Oxford, England*

The Historical Jesus and the Kerygmatic Christ

I

THE NEW TESTAMENT AS THE MYTHOLOGICAL AND INTERPRETATIVE CREATION OF THE PRIMITIVE CHRISTIAN COMMUNITIES

The expression "the quest of the historical Jesus" has become familiar to us as the English title of Albert Schweitzer's *Von Reimarus zu Wrede*. It has come to stand for the attempt to discover the personality and career of Jesus of Nazareth as a figure in human history by the application of modern methods of historical research to the New Testament writings. The attempt has ended, it is now generally agreed, in almost total failure.[1] It has served only to demonstrate that it is impossible to reconstruct a history of Jesus from the New Testament. For in these writings the only scientifically attainable object of historical research is not Jesus, but the first Christians believing in Jesus and interpreting him to others.[2] What we encounter here is not Jesus as he was in himself, but *what Jesus meant* to those who, after his death, continued to believe in him and his message. The complex amalgam of traditions which constitutes the New Testament grows out of, and is woven around a single central mes-

[1] For the fuller exposition of this point cf. J. Robinson, "The Impossibility and Illegitimacy of the Original Quest," in *A New Quest of the Historical Jesus* (London, 1959), p. 26.
[2] This is the characteristic position, for example, of J. Wellhausen, *Einleitung in die drei ersten Evangelien* (Berlin, ²1911).

sage: the *kerygma,* or apostolic proclamation of the inward and saving significance which, so the early Christians believed, Jesus bears for all men of all ages because of what God wrought in him, in what he once said and did, suffered and achieved.[3] In other words, the New Testament confronts us not with *the historical Jesus,* but with *the kerygmatic Christ,*[4] in whom God addresses a saving message to each individual, mediating it through this amalgam of interpretative traditions.

Now in order to express this inward eternal significance which they found in Jesus and sought to communicate, the first Christians had perforce to draw upon the basic views of God, man and the world available to them from their own cultural and religious backgrounds. These were complex and heterogeneous in character, but may broadly be divided into "Jewish-Palestinian" on the one hand, and "Gentile-Hellenistic" on the other.[5] Naturally the minds of the Jewish-Palestinian Christians were deeply conditioned by the Old Testament and by the apocalyptic and eschatological traditions of later Judaism: for instance, by the widespread Messianic expectation which immediately preceded the Christian era. Jesus himself would have been inspired by such eschatological hopes,[6] and after his death this apocalyptic element in his message would have been maintained and extended by his Jewish followers.

The Hellenistic converts to Christianity are also held to have interpreted Jesus in terms of their own basic preconceptions of

[3] For an explanation of the *kerygma* as the first exposition of the inward significance of Jesus, having as its central point his death and resurrection, cf. J. Robinson, *op. cit.,* pp. 38ff.

[4] Ever since this distinction was first formulated it has been fiercely debated how the one was related to the other. For a representative cross-section of the debate cf. H. Ristow and K. Matthiae (editors), *Der historische Jesus und der kerygmatische Christus* (Berlin, 1961), and on the "post-Bultmannian" phases of the debate, C. Braaten and R. Harrisville (editors), *The Historical Jesus and the Kerygmatic Christ: Essays on the New Quest of the Historical Jesus* (New York, 1964).

[5] On this distinction, and on the subsequent fusion of the two cultural influences cf. R. Bultmann, *Das Urchristentum im Rahmen der antiken Religionen* (Zürich, [2]1954). English translation: *Primitive Christianity in Its Contemporary Setting* (London/New York, 1956).

[6] Cf. R. Bultmann, *op. cit.,* pp. 86ff.

God, the universe and man, and of the relationships between them. The Judaism of the Diaspora (as distinct from that of Palestine) had already been open to the influence of Greek thought long before the Christian era. Philo had attempted to show, by a systematic process of allegorization of the Old Testament, that the riches of Greek philosophy were already buried and awaiting discovery in the ancient traditions of the Jews. In other ways, too, an intensely complex process of cultural interpenetration had been developing between the Jewish and Greek worlds.[7] But apart from this, it is held, traces of popular Stoicism and Neo-Platonism can be discerned in the more speculative of the New Testament writings, as well as the influence of such complex religious movements as those of Orphism and the Mystery religions.[8] Under such influences as these, the cultic and sacramental life of the Church became particularly important. Emphasis was laid on the belief that the risen Jesus was not merely awaited in his future *Parousia*, but was already rendered mystically present in the sacraments and in the cult.[9]

It should be recalled here that toward the end of the last century and the beginning of the present one the treasures of the Hellenistic world were being discovered with intoxicating swiftness, and the whole of antiquity was being ransacked for analogies with, and precedents for, the language, thought-forms and ideas of the New Testament. Thus, cults of divines of deified men and of dying and rising gods were alleged to have been found, as well as precedents for such doctrines as those of the Virgin Birth, and the activities of angelic or demonic powers.[10] Many such analogies have later been decisively discredited. Yet,

[7] Even in his treatment of "Hellenistic Judaism" (in *Primitive Christianity* . . . , pp. 94-100), Bultmann appears to underestimate the degree of this interpenetration. Cf., by way of comparison, T. Glasson, *Greek Influence in Jewish Eschatology* (London, 1961).

[8] Cf. R. Reitzenstein, *Die Hellenistischen Mysterienreligionen* (Leipzig/ Berlin, [3]1927). These Mystery religions are nowadays thought to have exercised virtually no influence whatever on Christian thought and practice.

[9] Cf. Bultmann, *Theology* . . . I, pp. 133ff.

[10] Cf. C. Clemen, *Religionsgeschichtliche Erklärung des Neuen Testaments* (Giessen, [2]1924).

they still represent a potent force in the interpretations of the "demythologizing" school, with which we are particularly concerned here. In this connection the influence of an alleged pre-Christian Gnosticism on Hellenistic, and also on certain branches of Jewish Christianity is especially important. For here, it is argued, is found a significant precedent for the concept of Jesus as preexistent Son of God and Savior. This is the famous myth of the "heavenly man" who descends to earth to rescue an enslaved humanity from its bonds by his saving word. His work of revelation completed, he ascends once more to heaven, thereby opening to all who receive his word a way by which they may follow him when released from this material world by death.[11] The kerygmatic Christ becomes, in the preaching of the Hellenists, a heavenly figure of this sort, and the preexistence of Jesus as divine Son of God in heaven becomes a key doctrine of Christianity.

It is clear, then, that the limitations of their various religious and cultural milieux compelled the first Christians to express the inward saving significance which they saw in Jesus in the form of stories, myths and legends about his earthly life. This is how Bultmann summarizes the message of the New Testament in its undemythologized form:

" 'In the fullness of time' God sent forth his Son, a preexistent divine being, who appears on earth as a man. He dies the death of a sinner on the cross and makes atonement for the sins of men. His resurrection marks the beginning of the cosmic catastrophe. Death, the consequence of Adam's sin, is abolished, and the daemonic forces are deprived of their power. The risen Christ is exalted to the right hand of God in heaven and made 'Lord' and 'King'. He will come again on the clouds of heaven

[11] Cf. H. Jonas, *Gnosis und spätantiker Geist I: Die mythologische Gnosis* (Göttingen, 1934). Bultmann relies heavily on this work. Yet today it is almost universally held that insofar as such a myth ever existed, it is found in texts later than those of Christianity and influenced by them. Cf. C. Colpe, *Die religionsgeschichtliche Schule. Darstellung und Kritik ihres Bildes vom gnostischen Erlösermythos* (Göttingen, 1961).

to complete the work of redemption, and the resurrection and judgment of men will follow. Sin, suffering and death will then be finally abolished. All this is to happen very soon; indeed, St. Paul thinks that he himself will live to see it." [12]

This message, the "demythologizers" maintain, is indeed ultimately rooted in the obscure historical events which culminated in Jesus' crucifixion. But as it now stands it is a tissue of myths and legends woven by the first Christians. In many cases we can actually recognize the Jewish or pagan sources of this mythology. Yet, it should not dismay us that this barrier of creative interpretation, which has been erected between us and the historical Jesus, has proved impenetrable to the scientific historians of our time. We should recognize with courageous enlightenment that the historical Jesus is not only lost beyond recovery, but is also, in spite of all appearances to the contrary, *almost totally irrelevant* to the deeper central meaning of the New Testament message.[13] We should bend all our resources to continuing and sustaining the *kerygma,* the proclamation of that essential saving significance which the Christians of the apostolic age first saw in Christ, which alone is still valid, and which still has a vital importance for the men of our times.[14]

The meaning of the kerygmatic Christ, then, (a) must be made available to modern scientific man in a form quite different from that in which it was originally promulgated, a form he can comprehend and accept. For this purpose (b) the tangled accumulations of tradition in which the essential message is embedded must be analyzed and interpreted. For the first of these tasks the method of form-criticism has been evolved, for the second, that of demythologizing.

[12] Cf. R. Bultmann, "New Testament and Mythology," in *Kerygma and Myth, a Theological Debate* (ed. H. Bartsch).

[13] Cf. Bultmann's famous statement that he does not know, and *does not wish to know,* anything about Jesus' own self-understanding, *Glauben und Verstehen* I (Tübingen, [1]1933), p. 101.

[14] Bultmann puts this point quite forcibly in his short popular monograph, *Jesus Christ and Mythology* (London, 1960). German translation, 1964.

II

FORM-CRITICISM AND "REDACTION HISTORY"
OF THE NEW TESTAMENT

We have seen that the failure to reconstruct the life of the historical Jesus has led to an intense, indeed exaggerated, emphasis on the creative activity of the post-Easter communities in forming the gospel tradition.[15] Literary criticism of the New Testament has tended independently in the same direction. The study of the complex interrelationships between the synoptic gospels had led to the classic "two-source" theory: the synoptic gospels as we now have them are derived from two sources, Mark and a source of sayings, Q. It was soon realized, however, that this was not enough. Each of these sources was itself complex, and evidently presupposed a long and complex process of evolution.

From the first the form-critics have maintained that both the topographical and chronological references in the gospel narratives are artificial and interpretative rather than historical.[16] It is, in effect, impossible to reconstruct the outward course of Jesus' life from the gospels. Consequently, the initial task of the form-critic is to recognize and set on one side the general redactional framework by means of which the originally isolated units of tradition were artificially fitted together in gospel form. What he is left with is a collection of the smallest and earliest units of tradition. With the exception of the Passion narratives these are nearly all extremely brief. They are classified, mainly by means of comparison with extra-biblical parallels, into a limited number of literary—or rather pre-literary—types. A preliminary division is drawn between discourse and narrative material. Then, according to Bultmann's system of classification,

[15] Cf. P. Benoit, "Reflexions sur la formgeschichtliche Méthode," in *Exégèse et Théologie I* (Paris, 1961), pp. 50ff.
[16] Cf. especially K. Schmidt, *Der Rahmen der Geschichte Jesu* (Berlin, 1919).

the discourses are divided as follows: (1) "Wisdom" sayings[17] (Matt. 6, 19-34); (2) Prophetic and apocalyptic sayings (e.g., Matt. 5, 3-9); (3) Legislative or disciplinary rules for the community (e.g., Matt. 18, 15-22); (4) The "I" sayings of Jesus (e.g., Mark 2, 17); (5) Parables and allegories. Bultmann also groups with this discourse material the *apophthegmata*, lapidary sayings of Jesus embodied in a narrative context. These are further subdivided into controversies and instructions (e.g., Mark 2, 1) and biographical *apophthegmata* (e.g., Mark 6, 1-6). The narrative material is divided into "miracle stories" and "historical narratives and legends".

The form-critic is now in a position to reconstruct the living context (*Sitz im Leben*) in the growth in the early Church in which such tradition units must have emerged. In the case of any given unit or type of unit he can decide how it reflects the ideals, or answers the exigencies of the particular group of early Christians which must have formulated it. To whom was it originally addressed? What reaction was it intended to produce? What were the special interests and characteristics of the group from which it emerged? The form-critic, however, does not confine himself to the earliest and most primitive stages in the formation of tradition. Between that earliest stage and the final crystallization in gospel form lies a whole series of intermediary stages in which the tradition-units are combined and recombined in various ways so as to form larger complexes of tradition in response to the developing needs of the community.[18]

Thus, the New Testament has come to be regarded as "the prayerbook of the primitive Church", created by a newly emerged and heterogeneous community of religious enthusiasts in the process of living out their ideals in a world always alien and usually hostile. The task these early Christians set themselves,

[17] Cf. R. Bultmann, *Die Geschichte der synoptischen Tradition* (Göttingen, ³1957). English translation: *The History of the Synoptic Tradition* (Oxford, 1963). For a brief summary cf. R. Bultmann and K. Kundsinn, *Form Criticism* (New York, 1962).

[18] Cf. especially "The Editing of the Spoken Word," in *The History of the Synoptic Tradition*, pp. 322ff.

it is said, was to create a pattern of ideal Christian living both for the internal life of the community (worship, catechesis, ethical teaching, maintenance of doctrinal orthodoxy, etc.), and for resisting or winning over those outside it (apologetic, religious authentication, condemnation of rival or older systems, steadfastness in persecution, political inoffensiveness, etc.). Thus, while the New Testament has its roots, obscure or for the most part quite invisible, in Jesus' life and death, it is created mainly by the primitive Christian communities, who authenticate their own idealized conceptions and interests by projecting them back into the life of their founder. In the gospels these ideals are expressed in story form, and in a manner typical of the environments in which they were created.

So far we have neglected the final redactional stage in the formation of the gospel traditions. Although Bultmann himself pays considerable attention to this,[19] the system of form-criticism as a whole undoubtedly emphasizes the earlier stages in the process to an excessive extent, and so exaggerates the creative role of the anonymous primitive Christian communities to a degree which is historically unrealistic. The recognition of this fact has led more recent scholars to concentrate on the final stage, hitherto neglected, at which the synoptic gospels acquire the form in which they now exist. These scholars examine the role of the individual evangelists and their distinctive ways of assembling and manipulating the material of earlier traditions. From this they deduce the distinctive theological interpretation which each evangelist gives to his particular gospel considered as a whole. Without actually superseding form-criticism, this "redaction history" is increasingly preoccupying contemporary New Testament scholars. Although it represents a salutary reaction against some of the excesses of form-criticism, it also concentrates attention upon a stage in the development of tradition which is still further removed from the historical Jesus than that of the primitive Christian communities.

An obvious and striking weakness of form-criticism is that it

[19] Cf. *The History* . . . , pp. 337ff.

grossly underestimates the capacity and intention of the New Testament writers to record historical facts about Jesus.[20] They were indeed concerned to apply the meaning of what Jesus had said and done to their own and their contemporaries' post-Easter situation. Their memories of Jesus were, no doubt, selected and arranged, presented and interpreted upon this principle. But they were presented quite unequivocally as real memories, the authenticity of which could be vouched for by still-living eye-witnesses.[21]

For some years Scandinavian and other scholars[22] have been exploring the techniques by which tradition was preserved and transmitted in rabbinical and Jewish circles. The New Testament traditions of Jesus, they contend, were preserved and transmitted in a similar manner. Their conclusions on this point are strikingly at variance with those of the form-critics. Indeed B. Gerhardsson's recent magisterial work on the subject[23] may well represent the most powerful challenge which form-criticism has ever had to face. Gerhardsson's most interesting conclusions are concerned with the faithful preservation of the "oral Torah", as distinct from the "written Torah", the biblical text, the purity of which was, of course, guarded with extreme care. In dealing with the oral Torah he first defines the categories of official exposition, *midrash* and *mishnah*, *halakah* and *haggadah*. He shows how not only the basic tradition, but also the explanation and discussion which grew up about it were preserved with scrupulous fidelity. Either the rabbi himself, or his immediate disciples, or later generations with fresh problems to solve might determine which elements of his words or conduct it was essen-

[20] Cf. P. Benoit, *op. cit.*, p. 47: "Peut-être les premiers chrétiens n'ont-ils pas eu le souci de l' "histoire", mais ils ont eu le souci de l' "historique".

[21] Cf. Acts 1, 21-22; 2, 32; 5, 32, etc.

[22] Cf. especially H. Riesenfeld, "The Gospel Tradition and Its Beginnings," in *The Gospels Reconsidered* (Oxford, 1960), pp. 131-53; cf. also J. Doeve, *Jewish Hermeneutics in the Synoptic Gospels* (Assen, 1954).

[23] B. Gerhardsson, *Memory and Manuscript. Oral Tradition and Written Transmission in Rabbinic Judaism and Early Christianity* (Copenhagen, 1961).

tial to retain. Official "repeaters", *tannaim,* were trained to learn and repeat these oral traditions by heart until they could be relied upon to transmit them with perfect accuracy. Sections of oral tradition were compressed into summaries, *kelalot,* containing the essential teaching of the rabbi on any given question. These in turn were remembered by their headings or titles, *simanim,* and mnemonic techniques were devised by which these *simanim* could be retained.

Evidence both from the New Testament itself and from the writings of the apostolic Fathers suggests that the tradition of Jesus and about Jesus was at first treated as oral Torah of this sort, the official written Torah still being the Old Testament. While the oral Torah of Jesus was still used with a certain freedom by the apostolic Fathers up to about 150 A.D., its authenticity is guaranteed by a carefully defined succession of official witnesses and transmitters reaching back to Jesus himself. Gerhardsson is careful to guard against the objection[24] that such methods of preservation and transmission were confined to esoteric circles of learned Jews, and were not representative of Judaism as a whole. On the contrary, he maintains that such techniques were well known and widespread, and argues that Jesus himself would have used them in transmitting what was essential in his message.

In spite of the hostile reception which his views have received from those of his reviewers who have vested interests in form-criticism, Gerhardsson's challenge is most impressive. So far it has not been seriously answered by the form-critics. Whatever revisions or modifications this theory may undergo in the course of time, it seems likely to lead to a radical revision of the categories of tradition in New Testament study. And it can hardly fail to reopen the way back from the New Testament to the historical Jesus. There is no reason why it should thereby destroy the kerygmatic Christ.

[24] Cf. his *Tradition and Transmission in Early Christianity* (Copenhagen, 1964).

III

The Interpretation of the New Testament: Demythologizing

From the problem of analyzing the New Testament traditions we turn to the problem of interpreting them, and specifically to that method of interpretation known as demythologizing. Bultmann's various explanations of demythologizing almost invariably commence with a statement of what modern, scientific, enlightened man finds unacceptable and incredible in the New Testament.[25] Basically it amounts to an assertion of the impossibility of supernatural or preternatural intervention in the world. But it is stated as baldly and dogmatically as any proposition in Denzinger's *Enchiridion Symbolorum*. For instance, according to Bultmann, the conception of the universe which the New Testament presupposes is that of a three-storied structure with heaven (the abode of God and the angels) above, hell (the dwelling of the demons) below, and earth (the habitat of man and the animals) between the two. This central sphere constitutes a sort of battleground, subject to invasion by the denizens of heaven and hell, who constantly intervene either benevolently or malevolently in the course of nature and history. But, objects modern man, science has established both in history and in the physical order an unbroken chain of causality, which does not admit of the intervention either of God and his angels, or of demons. The natural order cannot be ". . . interrupted or, so to speak, perforated, by supernatural powers".[26] Still less is man's interior spirit open to such invasions.

In what form, then, can this message about Jesus, pervaded as it is with uncompromising assertions of the supernatural, be accepted by modern man? For honesty compels him, if he accepts it at all, to accept it as a whole, without subtracting the

---

[25] Cf. his *New Testament and Mythology*, pp. 1ff.; *idem, Jesus Christ and Mythology*, pp. 14ff., etc.
[26] *Ibid.*, p. 15.

supernatural elements.[27] These considerations drive modern man to recognize the radically mythological character of the New Testament and to interpret it accordingly. Now mythology for Bultmann ". . . expresses a certain understanding of human existence". It is an expression necessarily inadequate, and necessarily cast in story form, of man's belief that ". . . the world and human life have their ground and limits in a power which is beyond all that we can calculate or control". Primitive man can express this "other-worldly" power as it affects him and his environment only by ascribing "this-worldly" status and activities to it. "Myths give worldly objectivity to that which is unworldly." [28] Applying this to the New Testament, we find that the climactic point of its message is unmistakably the death and resurrection of Jesus, in which God utters his saving word to men. This is considered as a single event, the "Christ event".[29] The rest of the New Testament unfolds the central significance of this Christ event in the oblique form of stories of Jesus' marvellous words and works. The task of demythologizing is to free this essential saving message of God from its mythological expression, and to reformulate it in terms appropriate to the philosophical outlook of our own times.

Modern man, then, does not have to do violence to his own reason by believing that the supernatural events recorded in the gospels took place in historical fact. Indeed, preoccupations with historical factuality distract him from the true object of faith, *the inward spiritual message* which the New Testament stories enshrine for him, as this applies to his own particular human situation. Certainly this inward message is ultimately rooted in two historical events: the event of Jesus' death on the cross and the event of his disciples' Easter faith in his resurrection. But it presents these events not as facts of history, but as God's *gesture,* summoning man to faith and obedience. A ges-

---

[27] *New Testament and Mythology*, p. 9: ". . . we cannot save the kerygma by selecting some of its features and subtracting others, and thus reducing the amount of mythology in it."

[28] *Jesus Christ and Mythology*, p. 19.

[29] Cf. *New Testament and Mythology*, pp. 33ff.

ture is a physical act or movement whose primary purpose is not to effect a physical change, but to communicate meaning. The gesture of God in the crucified Jesus conveys the meaning of dying to the world, and to the radically fallen, corrupt and sinful state in which man finds himself there. The meaning of this divine gesture is continued in the disciples' faith in Jesus' resurrection. For the resurrection represents mythologically that state of transcendent and authentic life which consists in living for the future which God graciously bestows upon man in word and promise. This is what it is to be risen from the dead.

This basic meaning of the death and resurrection of Jesus is explicitated and drawn to a sharp point in the *kerygma,* the preaching of the first Christians, and so thrusts into the life of every man, making the gracious and God-given future present to him in word and promise, and summoning him to decide, here and now, between God and the world, life and death, freedom and bondage. Man's decision to die to the world and to his own sins, and to live solely *by* God's word and *for* the future which that word makes present to him, must be sustained and constantly renewed in every moment of the believer's life.

The *kerygma,* then, is continuous with, and inseparable from, the Jesus who died and was believed to have risen in history, exactly as a word is continuous with, and inseparable from, the gesture which accompanies it or precedes it. Both together convey the same meaning. The New Testament writings progressively draw out the various aspects and implications of this central meaning in response to the needs, challenges and interests of the early Christian communities to whom they are addressed.

What does it matter, then, if these writings, which seem at first sight to be making a series of incredible historical assertions about Jesus' life on earth, turn out to be steeped in mythological ideas, full of internal inconsistencies and contradictions,[30] and manifestly irreconcilable with the scientific conclusions of modern physical and historical research? So far from being dismayed

[30] *Ibid.,* pp. 11-2.

by this discovery that the New Testament almost totally fails to convey a history of Jesus, the man of faith actually glories in it. He knows that faith, to be true faith, must be totally unsupported by intellectual evidence.[31] It is at its sharpest and purest when, with all the intellectually ascertainable facts against it, it says: "*Nevertheless* I believe; I accept and embrace, in total self-commitment, that message which, quite invisible to the eye of the scientific investigator, still shines out for me from this unscientific farrago of myth and legend."

In his conception of fallen man as totally corrupted by sin Bultmann is true to the classical tenets of Lutheranism. In his *a priori* rejection of the supernatural he appears to state more uncompromisingly, and to carry through more consistently than any of his predecessors, the characteristic attitude of Liberal Protestantism. In his stark refusal of all exterior rational support for the act of faith, his fideism approximates that of Barth. In his insistence upon the spiritual message immanent in the mythological material of the New Testament, he evidently stands close to Strauss. In certain significant respects his conception of faith also resembles Ritschl's.[32] Like Ritschl, Bultmann refuses to find any "theoretic" or "objectivizing" knowledge of God in the New Testament message. For what that message presents us with is God in his gratuitous and saving impact upon man fallen and helpless in his sins. And man's response of faith, according to Bultmann, consists in a decision, a choice between God and the world as the answer to his dire need.

But what chiefly distinguishes Bultmann's hermeneutical theory is the particular philosophical system he selects as providing the appropriate categories in which to convey the demythologized message of the New Testament to modern man. As Schleiermacher consciously used the philosophy of Spinoza, and Strauss that of Hegel in interpreting the New Testament, so Bultmann uses the existentialist principles of Heidegger[33] for the

[31] *Jesus Christ and Mythology*, pp. 60ff.
[32] A. Ritschl, *The Christian Doctrine of Justification and Reconciliation* (Edinburgh, 1900), p. 195.
[33] Cf. his *Sein und Zeit* (Tübingen, [10]1963). English translation: *Being*

same purpose. The central point of this philosophical system appears to be the distinction between *Vorhandensein,* that kind of "thing-like" being, or "being extant" which man shares with animals and with other material things, and *Dasein,* that specifically human form of existence in which man can reflect upon himself and his world, and make decisions of permanent and transcendent significance. For every man has his own unique history.[34]

Now with one important reservation, this existentialist conception of self-commitment to the future, this summons to exist as self in the face of death, provides exactly the category of thought which Bultmann needs in order to interpret the New Testament doctrine of the fall and the redemption. The New Testament also presents us with a picture of man as thrown down and helpless, even more radically helpless in his sin than the "self" of the existentialists, destined to a death which is even more absolute and accursed. Fallen man is totally incapable of achieving authentic life by any effort of his own. What, then, can avail to rescue him? Neither the self-assertion of the ancient Jews, which consists in self-righteous conformity to the law, nor the self-assertion of modern scientists, who seek to control the world and mold it to their will, nor yet the self-assertion of philosophers, which declares that man can transcend his fallen state by his own human powers, in deciding to commit himself to his own destiny. For Bultmann self-assertion is the sin of sins.[35] It is at the very point where man can do nothing—nothing at all—that God intervenes, freeing him from the state of sin which vitiates his own past, summoning him and empowering him to commit himself by faith to the eschatological future of life in Christ. "Here, then, is the crucial distinction between the New Testament and existentialism, between the Christian faith

---

and Time (London, 1962). For a brief and lucid explanation of this philosophy cf. L. Malevez, *Le Message chrétien et le mythe: La théologie de Rudolph Bultmann* (Paris, 1954), pp. 25ff.

[34] For an analysis of what Bultmann means cf. especially *Glauben und Verstehen* II (Tübingen, 1952), pp. 1-19.

[35] *New Testament and Mythology,* p. 30.

and the natural understanding of Being. The New Testament speaks, and faith knows, of an act of God through which man becomes capable of self-commitment, capable of faith and love, of his authentic life." [36]

IV

THE NEW QUEST OF THE HISTORICAL JESUS

For Bultmann the "Christ event" in which the gesture of God takes place is almost entirely confined to the death and resurrection of Jesus. He resolutely refuses to trace the historical roots of the New Testament *kerygma* further back into Jesus' earthly life. This refusal seems both arbitrary and unrealistic. Surely, in defining the *kerygma,* it is only reasonable to take into account the manifest and explicit intentions of those who first proclaimed it. Now the moment one adverts to this *intention of the original tradents,* it becomes, in effect, impossible to deny that they meant to convey to their hearers certain real facts of Jesus' earthly ministry. Possibly in view of this, several of Bultmann's pupils have initiated a "new quest of the historical Jesus".[37] While the old quest for his personality and biographical details remains for them futile and irrelevant, they do find it possible and necessary to penetrate back through the *kerygma* not merely to Jesus on the cross, but to Jesus in the whole span of his public life, that is, to the historical Jesus *considered precisely in his existential significance.*

As J. M. Robinson puts it, "His action, the intention latent in it, the understanding of existence it implies, and thus his selfhood, can be encountered historically." [38] E. Käsemann, the initiator of this new quest, argues that while the first Christians were incapable of abstracting from their faith in their presentation of Jesus' history, they were equally incapable of setting up

[36] *Ibid.,* p. 33.
[37] Cf. J. M. Robinson, *op. cit.,* and R. Fuller, *The New Testament in Current Study* (Scribner, 1962), pp. 33-67.
[38] Cf. J. M. Robinson, *op. cit.,* p. 105.

a myth in the place of history, or of allowing a heavenly being to stand in the place of the Nazarene. From very early times they had to combat in their hearers not only an exaggeratedly human interest in Jesus, but also the opposite Docetist tendency of reducing his humanity to mere appearance. It is particularly true of Luke that he intended to present his readers with the life of the earthly Jesus. The fourth gospel too, stemming as it does from the time of the anti-Docetist controversies, resolutely upholds the view that revelation took place in the earthly ministry of Jesus as well as in the culminating events of his life.[39]

H. Conzelmann[40] points to a number of features in the gospel narrative which are unique, and which set Jesus in sharp contrast both to the milieu in which his life was allegedly spent, and to that in which the gospels were written. Thus, even though during the relevant period Palestine was surrounded and interpenetrated with Greek cities (*e.g.*, Sepphoris, which was barely two kilometers from Nazareth), the movement initiated by Jesus seems, in its early stages, to have been remarkably unaffected by Hellenism. It is manifestly Jewish, and seems to be a messianic movement which, like the sectarian movement of Qumran, arose in emancipation from, and in opposition to, the more official circles of Judaism. Yet, in its universal appeal to sinners, in its message of forgiveness and faith, and in its radical anti-legalism, this movement is diametrically opposed to the sectarianism of Qumran, and appears, when compared with any other known form of Judaism, quite unique. It even differs in important respects from the closely related movement of the Baptist. John had called people from their cities out into the desert with the summons, "Repent, for the kingdom of heaven is at hand!" (Matt. 3, 2). Their repentance and conversion were manifested in ascetic practices. Jesus sought out his fellow Jews in their own cities with the same summons, but his mission was not

[39] E. Käsemann, "Das Problem des historischen Jesus," in *Zeitschrift für Theologie und Kirche* (1954), pp. 125-53; reprinted in *Exegetische Versuche und Besinnungen* I (Göttingen, 1960), pp. 187-214.

[40] "Jesus Christus," in *Die Religion in Geschichte und Gegenwart* III ([3]1959), cols. 619-53.

ascetic. His followers were to rely neither on the false security of belonging to the chosen people, nor on the equally false security of ascetic works. Their security was to rest solely on faith in the God whose loving and forgiving attitude toward them in their sins was revealed in Jesus' own merciful words and works.

Again a number of elements can be discerned which must, of their nature, refer to a unique and unrepeatable situation in Jesus' own life, and which cannot reflect any typical situation in the life of the post-Easter community. Such elements cannot reasonably be explained as retrospective creations of the community, intended to authenticate some characteristic practice or belief of its own.[41] The authenticity of a number of Jesus' sayings is further confirmed by the fact that they are demonstrably Aramaic in origin. This would apply to a substantial nucleus of the parables.

Even allowing for the scientific scepticism of modern historians, it is clear that Jesus did indeed appear as prophet and lawgiver, wonder-worker and teacher, his works complementing and reinforcing his words, and together constituting a meaningful and powerful encounter in the here and now with God as gracious and pardoning. He comes as the last summoner of all, and proclaims the coming of God's kingdom in such a way that it becomes real in his own gracious works of healing the sick, blessing the poor, and forgiving sinners. In his own basic attitude and behavior,[42] in his bold assault upon legalism, in his sovereign authority, by which he proclaims pardon for publicans and harlots and judgment for the righteous, and finally in his humble submission to God's will, Jesus makes the future kingdom of God already proleptically present.

[41] Ibid., col. 623.
[42] Cf. E. Fuchs, Studies in the Historical Jesus (S.T.B.42) (London, 1954).

CONCLUSION

Apart from the obvious inadmissability of the rationalist dogma that the supernatural is impossible, we may mention three classic objections to Bultmann's position which have never been answered entirely satisfactorily.[43]

1. The existentialist "prior understanding" (*Vorverständnis*) with which Bultmann deliberately approaches the New Testament prejudices his exposition of its meaning, causes him to neglect the numerous elements in it which are not susceptible of an existentialist interpretation, and acts as a "Procrustes' bed", truncating and distorting the message of the New Testament as a whole.

2. Bultmann's interpretation of the "salvation event" makes it too dependent upon the believer. The crucifixion and resurrection of Jesus become the salvation event only when they are proclaimed as such in the *kerygma,* and received as such by those who respond to it with the decision of faith, thereby allowing themselves to be raised to eschatological existence.

3. In his concentration on the martyr's death of Jesus, Bultmann has often been accused of Docetism; he seems to reduce the Savior to a mere salvation event. Could not the meaning he finds in this equally be educed from the martyr's death of that earlier preacher of the coming kingdom of God, the Baptist? [44] In what *unique* sense is God "in" Jesus? Why, indeed, is it necessary to locate the saving message of God in any earthly event at all? Is not the logical consequence of Bultmann's position really that the historical Jesus can be dispensed with altogether? Why should not this historical event be demythologized along with the rest of the "historically objectivizing" statements of the New Testament, which are liable to distract one from the keryg-

[43] For a discussion of these first two objections cf. Fuller, *The New Testament in Current Study, op. cit.,* pp. 25ff.

[44] On this line of objection cf. the excellent article of G. Ladd, "The Role of Jesus in Bultmann's Theology," in *Scottish Journal of Theology* 18 (1965), pp. 66ff.

matic summons to the decision of faith? Or, if we regard Jesus as the bearer of the word, in what sense is this word uniquely "in" Jesus? Is he unique merely in the sense that he is the first of a long series of men who are instruments of the word, many of them, like Jesus himself, witnessing to the word they preached with their life's blood?

Despite all the deeply false and heretical aspects of Bultmann's theories, the entire Christian world should be grateful to him and to his pupils. Christians have learned from him to concentrate not on the external, material factuality, but on the deep theological meaning of Jesus, to regard his life, death and resurrection as God's meaningful gesture whose eternal saving significance is explicitated and reinforced by Jesus' own words, and by the words of the post-Easter *kerygma.* Yet we cannot stop there. We must regard the "event" of Jesus, from his incarnation to his resurrection, not merely as a gesture, but as a *sacramental* gesture. Like the pouring of the water at baptism, it *effects what it signifies.* It *causes* that redemption, that re-creation, that life of grace, that present promise of future bliss which is proclaimed in the *kerygma,* extending these to the men of all ages from the glorified, yet still physical body of the risen Christ. It is this specifically Catholic principle of sacramentality which makes the *historical Jesus,* in his concrete factuality, one and continuous with the *kerygmatic Christ* in his eternal saving meaningfulness.

Piet Schoonenberg, S.J./ *Nijmegen, Netherlands*

"He Emptied Himself" Philippians 2, 7

Since Chalcedon our theology has expressed the plenitude of Christ by attributing two natures to him, divine and human. When, however, we look from this theological point of view to the witness of Christ in the writings of the New Testament, we do indeed find the plenitude but not the duality of later dogmatic teaching. We discover instead another duality, more "horizontal", that of Jesus' life on earth and of his presence in heaven, the condition of the "servant" and his power, his self-emptying and his exaltation. I hope that this article, which deals with the self-emptying, the *kenosis,* will show the importance of incorporating also this other duality in our theological thinking. After a brief exegetical analysis of this subject I shall suggest a theological approach which, needless to say, is but an attempt in this direction. I am trying to arrive at an understanding, within our faith, of the earthly existence of the Christ who exists for all ages.

SELF-EMPTYING AND EXALTATION IN THE SCRIPTURES

In its most simple form the oldest kerygma is: "Jesus is Lord" (1 Cor. 12, 3; Phil. 2, 11). This confession coincides with belief in his resurrection (Rom. 10, 9). Only after his resurrection is Jesus "made Lord and Christ" (Acts 2, 36). This does not mean that the earthly life of Jesus was without significance for salvation. On the contrary, the earliest preaching and the gospels show more and more clearly that not only his death on the cross but all his words and actions on earth were seen in the light of the saving power of his lordship. In St. John's gospel he is from the beginning God's own Word. And yet, throughout the whole New Testament there remains the awareness of a difference between Jesus on earth and Christ in heaven.

This difference finds a more or less concrete expression in the titles "Lord" and "servant". Christ's life on earth and his death are seen as the fulfillment of the image of Yahweh's servant, of the four songs in Deutero-Isaiah (Is. 42, 1-9; 49, 1-11; 50, 4-11; 52, 13—53, 12); the same holds for the earliest preachers (Acts 8, 32-35; 1 Peter 2, 21-25) and the authors of the gospels. It is not improbable that Jesus himself found his life's mission expressed in the image of the servant. It is particularly important to remember that the image of the servant appears both at the beginning of Jesus' preaching and when he enters upon his passion.

In the synoptics Jesus' preaching is preceded by the passages about his baptism in the Jordan. The words addressed there by the Father to Jesus echo the words with which God introduces his servant in the first song: "Behold my servant, whom I uphold, my chosen, in whom my soul delights" (Is. 42, 1). After this baptism, Jesus himself, in all probability, and the evangelists certainly, see his task as that of the servant of Yahweh. John makes even the Baptist recall the final sacrifice of the servant's life: "Behold, the lamb of God, who takes away the sin of the world" (John 1, 29; cf. Is. 53, 7 and 11). When the time for this sacrifice approaches, the image of the servant again appears in the answer to the mother of the sons of Zebedee, and in the quarrel that follows: "For the Son of Man also has not come to be served but to serve, and to give his life as a ransom for many" (Mark 10, 45 = Matt. 20, 28).

The end of the servant's prophetic mission, which is to give his life for the many (Is. 53, 11), is now clearly expressed. Luke puts this scene at the last supper and ends with the words: "But I am in your midst as he who serves" (Luke 22, 27), while John illustrates it in the washing of the feet (John 13, 1-17). The references to the servant appear, moreover, even in the institution of the eucharist. Although the synoptics describe the last supper as a paschal meal, Jesus' words at the institution do not allude to the paschal lamb but to the sacrifice of the servant.[1]

Whenever this image of the servant appears, it is linked either with Jesus' existence as the gentle prophet exposed to contradiction (the narratives of his temptation in Matthew and Luke show how much Jesus prefers this role to that of a spectacular Messiah) or with his suffering. In brief, the image of the servant always points to the opposite of glory, to a self-emptying. This self-emptying or *kenosis* is described extensively in Philippians 2, 6-11. Many biblical scholars hold that this text is an original hymn of the early Church, quoted by Paul. I give the text here in strophic sections; the line in brackets seems to be an insertion by Paul himself.

> Christ Jesus, who, though he was in the form of God,
> did not count equality with God a thing to be grasped.
> He emptied himself,
> taking the form of a servant,
> being born in the likeness of men.
> And being found in human form
> he humbled himself
> and became obedient unto death
> [even to death on a cross].
> Therefore God has highly exalted him
> and bestowed on him the name
> which is above every name,
> that at the name of Jesus
> every knee should bow,

[1] Cf. J. Betz, *Die Eucharistie in der Zeit der griechischen Väter* II/1 (Freiburg, 1961), pp. 26-35.

in heaven and on earth and under the earth,
and every tongue confess
that Jesus Christ is Lord,
to the glory of God the Father.

This hymn, particularly the first half, has for long been the subject of much controversy among biblical scholars and theologians.[2] It begins by mentioning Jesus' divine form or existence. The first verse also mentions "equality with God". Curiously enough, this is expressed in an adverbial phrase: *einai isa*—not: *ison Theō*, so that we may translate it also as "life on a divine level" or "living in a divine state". And it is said that Christ did not consider this *harpagmon* (robbery). This word may mean "robbery" in the active sense, though here it means more probably "what is robbed", or "booty" in the passive sense.

This can again be understood as something already acquired or as something still to be acquired. If taken as "already acquired" the text means that Jesus did not cling to it. If taken as "still to be acquired", then it means that he does not try to grasp it. This seems to me the most probable interpretation, particularly because of the parallels in the gospels: Jesus' choice at the moment of temptation and at the approach of his passion.

So Christ does not try to grasp "life on a divine level" while he is still on earth. "But he emptied himself" (*alla heauton ekenō-sen*). If Jesus already possessed this life on a divine level, then this must be precisely what he emptied himself of. But if such a life was not yet in his possession, then the "emptying" can be understood in an absolute sense: he emptied himself, reduced himself to nothing (for this interpretation, cf. 1 Cor. 1, 17; 9, 15; Rom. 4, 14). This Jesus did by taking the existence—here again, the form, *morphē*—of a servant. Is there an allusion here to man as God's servant, to the just of Israel, to the prophets or to the servant of Deutero-Isaiah? Perhaps to all of them. In this

[2] Cf. P. Henry, "Kenose," in *Dictionnaire de la Bible Supplement* (Paris: Letouzey et Ane, 1957) V, cols. 7-161. In my exegesis I have made much use of A. Feuillet, "L'Homme-Dieu considéré dans sa condition terrestre de Serviteur et de Rédempteur," in *Vivre et Penser* (War edition of *Revue Biblique*), 2nd. ser., I (1942), pp. 58-79.

case, becoming equal to man may be a further explanation of the
"servant" or refer to the refusal of Yahweh's servant to put himself above men. But here, as in the relation toward God, there
is no question of an equality of nature or essence; it is rather a
matter of equality in the way of life and the pattern of behavior
(*skēmati, habitu*). This fitting into our human, earthly existence
is then fully developed in the third verse. He humbled himself,
and in this we can hear that renunciation of divine equality. He
did this in obedience, evidently to a divine mission, like the
servant of Yahweh. And this obedience lasted unto death; in
the light of Paul's addition we may say: unto and in death.
After this death, however, God exalted his servant highly (*hy-
perypsōsen*). This exaltation is described in the second part of
the hymn, which concentrates on Jesus' heavenly state as Lord,
to the glory of the Father.

In some texts Paul himself sees Jesus' earthly life as one
whole, and then it is again a "self-emptying", although expressed
in different words. The opposite of this emptying may already
be called a divine preexistence in Paul: "Though he was rich,
yet for your sake he became poor, so that by his poverty you
might become rich" (2 Cor. 8, 9). This poverty is the "emptying" of divine riches, just as the "form of the servant" is the
emptying of divine majesty. It means an equality with man as
servant and so an equality in the tutelage of God's people while
they were still under the law: "But when the time had fully
come, God sent forth his Son, born of woman, born under the
Law, to redeem those who were under the law, so that we might
receive adoption as sons" (Gal. 4, 4-5). Christ also took upon
himself the curse of the law to turn it into our blessing: "Christ
redeemed us from the curse of the law, having become a curse
for us" (Gal. 3, 13). The law and its curse could affect Christ
because his existence stood in the sign of our sin: "For God has
done what the law, weakened by the flesh, could not do: sending
his own Son in the likeness of sinful flesh and for sin, he con-
demned sin in the flesh, in order that the just requirement of the
law might be fulfilled in us, who walk not according to the flesh
but according to the Spirit" (Rom. 8, 3-4). In one word—and

a very strong word at that—"For our sake he made him to be sin who knew no sin, so that in him we might become the righteousness of God" (2 Cor. 5, 21).

As in the hymn of Philippians 2, 6-11, so in the epistle to the Hebrews the humiliation and passion of Christ rest upon his own choice: "Who for the joy that was set before him endured the cross, despising the shame, and is seated at the right of the throne of God" (Heb. 12, 2). This choice may have occurred in the earthly life of Jesus, when "in every respect he has been tempted as we are" (Heb. 4, 15). But the beginning of this life, Christ's coming into this world, was linked with such a choice: "Consequently, when Christ came into the world, he said, 'Sacrifices and offerings thou hast not desired, but a body hast thou prepared for me; in burnt offerings and sin offerings thou hast taken no pleasure.' Then I said, 'Lo, I have come to do thy will, O God,' as it is written of me in the roll of the book" (Heb. 10, 5-7; Ps. 40, 7-9).

This conscious entering into the world implies preexistence on Christ's part, and this belief is expressed at the beginning of the epistle where Christ is called "the Son . . . through whom also he created the world" (Heb. 1, 2). In the light of this pre-existence, two phases of Christ's human existence are described, one on earth, marked above all by the cross, and the other in heaven: "When he had made purification for sins, he sat down at the right hand of the Majesty on high" (Heb. 1, 3). These two phases are described in various ways. "Jesus, who for a little while was made lower than the angels, (was) crowned with glory and honor" because God "wanted to make (him) perfect through suffering" (Heb. 2, 9). "In the days of his flesh, Jesus offered up prayers and supplications, with loud cries and tears, to him who was able to save him from death, and he was heard for his godly fear. Although he was the Son, he learned obedience through what he suffered; and being made perfect he became the source of eternal salvation to all who obey him, being designated by God a high priest after the order of Melchizedek" (Heb. 5, 7-10).

In John, more than in the other evangelists, the majesty of the eternal Word and the final glory of the risen Christ permeate the life of Jesus on earth. But even here the unfinished and "emptied" condition of Christ on earth stands out sharply against this background, as, for example, where John the Baptist calls Jesus the "Lamb of God, that takes away the sin of the world".[3] Or again where the unbelief that Jesus encounters is linked with the suffering servant (John 12, 39 = Is. 53, 1).

The most striking illustration, however, of the Lord as the servant is given in the passage where Christ washes the feet of his disciples, "knowing that the Father had given all things into his hands, and that he had come from God and was going to God" (John 13, 3). The word "servant" is not applied in this passage to Christ himself, who calls himself rather "Teacher and Lord" (13, 13). But the contrast between this true title and Jesus' action accurately recalls the same thought as that "taking the form of a servant" of Philippians 2, 6-11. And so the conclusion of the scene in John runs in the same vein—like the Lord, we also ought to wash one another's feet (John 13, 14-16). John also brings out the thought that the "emptied" condition does not merely refer to the position of Jesus as an individual but above all to the salvation he applies to us: during his life on earth Jesus is not yet he who sends the Spirit; this he is, only when he is with the Father (John 7, 39 and 16, 7). Thus the evangelist who insists most on Christ's glory also gives us the clearest description of his "emptying".

THEOLOGICAL DISCUSSION

In general, Catholic theology does not deal extensively with the subject of Christ's *kenosis*. High Scholasticism used to treat

---

[3] Or is *amnos* in John 1, 29 and 35 a wrong translation of the Aramaic *talia*, which means "boy" or "servant"? Cf. J. Jeremias, "amnos" and "pais" in *Theologisches Wörterbuch zum Neuen Testament;* other authors are mentioned by M.-E. Boismard, "Du Baptême à Cana," in *Lectio Divina* 18 (Paris, 1956), pp. 46f.

of the mysteries of Jesus' life on earth: birth, baptism, temptations, transfiguration, etc. The aspect of *kenosis* did not quite
receive its full measure in all this, and, in any case, the treatment
of these mysteries disappeared from christological treatises ages
ago. *Kenosis* appears in the question about Christ's *passibilitas,
i.e.,* the question whether it is possible for the God-Man to suffer.

Where this question is not limited to the actual passion of
Christ but is seen as a permanent condition of Christ during his
whole life on earth, as in M. Scheeben's *Dogmatik,*[4] the discussion is dominated by the preexistence of the Word. When one
starts from this point one will obviously see everything in Christ's
earthly life, including its imperfection and the slow growth mark-
ing all human life on this earth, as the "emptying" of the glory
that belongs to Christ as God's Son also, and permanently, in
his human condition. This glory is then seen as that of Adam in
paradise or as the fulfillment in the paradise of heaven.

The Son of God renounces this glory by assuming human
nature: it would have been possible for him to assume this
human nature in the condition of glory, but he chose to take
on the human condition in its humiliation. All the same, the
glory is not totally lacking: from the first moment of his human
existence he enjoys the human beatific vision. His life on earth
is therefore not only that of man "on the way" or "in progress",
the *viator,* but also that of man in his final perfection, the *comprehensor.*

This combination of the *viator* and the *comprehensor* created
many difficulties in theology, particularly in connection with the
possibility of Christ's suffering. Scheeben can cope with the
bodily suffering and the mortality of the God-Man, but he cannot explain his spiritual suffering on natural grounds. He man-
ages to localize this suffering on the periphery of the soul, leaving
the beatific vision and the full joy of heaven, which this vision
implies, in the center. But the fact that this joyous vision does

---

[4] M. Scheeben deals extensively with Christ's condition of *kenosis* in
his *Handbuch der katholischen Dogmatik,* V, chap. 3, part 3, §§254-9
(= *Gesammelte Schriften* VI/2 (Freiburg, 1954), pp. 108-56, esp. §256,
on pp. 121-7.

not permeate the whole of Christ's soul is a miracle for Scheeben. One might even say that in this view, apart from the ordinary miracles of Jesus, which show a revelation and a "breakthrough" of his glory (cf. John 2, 11), there is still the other "miracle", necessary to explain why this glorious and joyous vision does *not* break through in the life of Christ's soul.

These two facts together throw a surprising light on Christ's relation toward others, but are we entitled to call the second fact (of the glory not breaking through in Christ's inner life) a miracle, in the sense of an exception to the normal and natural course of things? The answer to this question seems to me to be negative and I would like to suggest a very different interpretation of Christ's *kenosis* on earth. The difference lies principally in the starting point. I prefer not to start from the preexistence of the Son.

The writings of the New Testament describe Jesus' life on earth from the memory of those who were then with him, and this memory cannot be separated from their experience of his glorified presence. Christ's life on earth was not, and cannot be, approached from any other angle. The preexistence of the Word within the divinity is not a direct object of the scriptural proclamation, and it can never be the direct object of our discussion. I do not want to say anything, therefore, about the incarnation of the Word itself, but will limit myself to the description of a choice falling within Jesus' life on earth. This will prompt another view of what he chooses. I may perhaps summarize my opinion under three headings:

(1) I do not see the choice of the path of *kenosis* as an act of the Son at the incarnation, but as a decision taken by the Son made man.

(2) This choice does not concern the renunciation of a human existence to which the Son of God is entitled, but rather a renunciation of what we, men, imagine to be the life of God's Son.

(3) In a positive sense, this choice was the acceptance by Jesus of his human condition in a situation determined by the

unbelief he encountered. I would like to explain each of these points.

1. The texts from the New Testament, analyzed above, clearly mention a choice, made by Jesus, between two ways of life: in the desert he rejects the way suggested by Satan; he defends his acceptance of suffering against Peter; he says he is come, not to be served, but to serve; he does not pursue an equality with God, but chooses the existence of a servant; he takes up the cross instead of the joy he is entitled to; he does not prefer his own will, but the chalice that his Father gives him to drink. Some texts place this choice at a specific moment of his life, as when he enters upon his passion. All these texts, however, can be understood of a decision taken within the limits of Jesus' human existence. This holds also for the hymn of Philippians 2, as has already been indicated. In other words, there is no need to understand the choice of this "self-emptying" as made by the Word at the moment of his incarnation; the texts apply just as well to a decision or decisions taken within the human existence of Jesus.

This last suggestion suits the texts even better. In Philippians 2, 7ff., one may see a double choice made by Jesus during his existence on earth: at the beginning of his preaching he "took upon himself the form of a servant (of *the* servant)", and at the approach of his suffering "he humbled himself and became obedient unto death". The narratives of the temptation in the synoptics are best understood as a summary of Jesus' decisions throughout his public life, particularly when, at the prospect of the passion, Peter himself becomes a "Satan" for him (Mark 8, 33). Paul's words, too, about the poverty that Christ took on and about his becoming a curse and sin, apply to this whole life in the light of his passion.

That he lived under the law and in the form of sinful flesh applies to his whole life on earth from the moment of his incarnation, but the choice of all this is ascribed by Paul, not to the Son becoming man, but to the Father who sends his Son (Gal. 4, 4; Rom. 8, 3). The letter to the Hebrews clearly refers to

Christ's earthly life when it says that he learns obedience and offers up prayers with loud cries and tears, in the Garden of Olives or on Golgotha (Heb. 5, 7ff.); his choice of the cross instead of joy (Heb. 12, 2) cannot be understood otherwise. It is true that in one passage (Heb. 10, 5-9) this letter mentions a sacrificial prayer of Christ himself "when he came into the world". This may have been inspired by the words of the Psalm (40, 7, Septuagint) which say: "Thou hast given me a body"; apart from this, Christ makes no choice between two ways of life on coming into the world.

Almost all the texts, therefore, that mention Christ's *kenosis,* show that he made this choice during his human existence. A negative proof can be found in John's prologue which deals with the incarnation in itself, indeed as becoming flesh, but without mentioning the flesh of sin, the humiliation, the *kenosis* or the form of the servant; instead it stresses the glory that the only-begotten Son receives from the Father (John 1, 14). We may therefore conclude that the *kenosis* is not the divine act of the Son at the incarnation but the choice made by the Word already made flesh during his earthly existence. Obviously, it is not an act of Christ's humanity only. The divine person of Christ, God's Son, "one of the Trinity", himself chooses the path of *kenosis* just as he himself suffers and dies on the cross. But this choice already presupposes his human existence. That is why this same humanity of Christ will not vanish at his death, but will be glorified.

2. Having defined more accurately exactly who chose the *kenosis,* we can now describe more accurately the *object* of this choice. In his humanity the Son of God chooses between two ways of human existence; he rejects the one and accepts the other. What does he reject? It may be useful to say first how this question should *not* be answered. First of all, Christ does not reject his divine nature. The kenotic theories, which suggested something like this in a kind of inverted monophysitism, are no longer accepted.[5] But if there were something in the hypothesis

[5] The theories are summarized by, among others, J. Ternus, "Chalke-

that God's presence as the Word only *becomes*[6] the personal Son in the man Jesus, then the *kenosis* as earthly imperfection of Christ and his glorification as perfection and therefore as full personalization would become meaningful for God's Son himself.

In this perspective it becomes significant that the words of the Psalm (2, 7): "You are my Son, today I have begotten you", are linked in two places of the New Testament with the resurrection of Jesus (Acts 13, 33) or his fulfillment or glorification (Heb. 1, 4-5). On the other hand, the gospels recognize Jesus also during his human life as the Son of God, standing, beyond all men, in a unique relation to the Father (Matt. 11, 27 par.; John 5, 19-26, etc.). If Jesus is on a level that is essentially higher than any other men sent or sanctified by God, it is necessary that, from the beginning and throughout his human existence, he must have been the Son in a divine manner. The resurrection did not simply make him the Son, but "designated" him "Son of God in power" (Rom. 1, 4). Although, therefore, his divine sonship may possibly be seen as "becoming" during his life on earth, he could not reject it because he *was* the Son. The same must be said of all that is implied in this divine sonship: the complete dedication to God, his unique mission and love, his sinlessness. Here we can speak still more justifiably of growth, not only in outward manifestation but also inwardly. But this growth takes place within the unique sanctity that Christ cannot reject because it, too, belongs to his being.

In this perspective one can compare Christ's earthly life and the situation in paradise as it is attributed to the first human

don und die Entwicklung der protestantischen Theologie," in *Das Konzil von Chalkedon* III, ed. A. Grillmeier and H. Bacht (Würzburg, 1954), pp. 531-611. They are rejected *en passant* by Pius XII in his encyclical *Sempiternus Rex,* Sept. 8, 1951.

[6] "The pronouns 'I', 'thou' and 'he' are given their clear, properly human significance in God through the incarnation of the Son," says E. Schillebeeckx in his "Het bewustzijnsleven van Christus," in *Tijdschrift voor Theologie* I (1961), pp. 227-51, esp. 242, n. 19. About the possibility that God's being becomes "three-personal" (trinitarian) *without further qualification* only in Christ and the Spirit when poured out, see P. Schoonenberg, "Over de Godmens," in *Bijdragen* 25 (1964), pp. 166-86.

beings in classical treatises of dogma. It is possible to maintain that this paradisal situation belongs properly to God's Son but that he rejected it. I would rather suggest that this paradisal condition not only belongs to Christ but was a reality in his life on earth. But then I mean this in a sense that differs radically from the "original justice" of classical theology.[7] I mean that integrity (*integritas*) should be stripped of all physical elements and placed wholly within grace itself. *Integritas* does not change man biologically or structurally or according to a nature that is contrasted to the person as a precondition, but personally, insofar as the person seizes control of his nature. *Integritas,* then, is nothing but the "personalizing", unifying, liberating, whole-making aspect of grace itself. It liberates man from his impulses so that these do not develop into "lust"; he is even free from death itself, for death becomes the entering upon final fulfillment.[8]

Such "integrity" is present insofar as it is not hampered by sin or its consequences and so can permeate us totally. It can therefore be considered present at the beginning of humanity as long as sin was not yet present. But it must be added at once that the innocence of mankind in its beginning, like that of a child, is, first of all, difficult to locate (where does our choice become morally good or bad?), and secondly, that this innocence is still immature, not yet stable and not yet fully personal. At the beginning of mankind, therefore, this "integrity" is still almost exclusively a promise; the "paradise" of Genesis 2 is what awaits us rather than what we have lost. But in Christ there is no

---

[7] K. Rahner puts *integritas* in the possibility given to us as persons to dominate human "nature" (*Vorhandenheit*) from within: "Zur theologischen Begriff der Konkupiszenz," in *Schriften zur Theologie* I (Einsiedeln, ²1956) pp. 377-414, esp. 402-5. English translation: *Theological Investigations* Vol. 1: *God, Christ, Mary and Grace* (Helicon, 1961). But this possibility arises from grace itself and is present in the degree in which grace dominates: P. Schoonenberg, "Zonde der wereld en erfzonde," in *Bijdragen* 24 (1963), pp. 350-86, esp. 380ff. English translation in *Man and Sin* (London, 1965).

[8] Cf. E. Schillebeeckx, *op. cit.,* pp. 248f., n. 6. For the theology of Jesus' knowledge and consciousness during his earthly life, see the article by E. Gutwenger in this volume.

personal sin to obstruct this "integrity", although he does stand in a sinful world.

On the one hand, therefore, we must attribute to him all the labor and pain of a human condition that grows and is mortal, to which the first human beings were also subject, and, on the other hand, all the suffering inflicted on him by our sin, until (and including) the death on the cross. It is precisely in this that he is the "integral", free, personal man who is not torn apart and who can bear all this to the full in obedience to his Father's mission and in utter love for us.

The blessing of final fulfillment, too, Christ cannot reject; but in this case it is because he does not possess it and it does not belong to him in his life on earth. The Son of God is truly entitled to glory and bliss, even in his humanity, but why should he not first follow the way toward it like every other man? It seems to me that otherwise his "being human" is not quite authentic and certainly not *our* way of being human.

In any case, theologians do not maintain that the Son of God had to assume a humanity in the state of fulfillment. If he is declared *comprehensor* (in the state of beatific vision), the reason—certainly in St. Thomas (*Summa Theologiae* III, q. 9, a. 2) —is that, being the source of our beatific vision, Christ must possess it himself. But this argument applies to Christ only when he has reached his final fulfillment. That is why, in spite of his unique consciousness of being the only-begotten Son, Christ did not have to enjoy on this earth a vision whose beatific quality would make his earthly suffering impossible and whose total comprehension would make any increase in knowledge superfluous. On this earth, therefore, Jesus was *viator*, no doubt in a unique manner because he is already the one who leads us toward life and salvation (Acts 3, 15; Heb. 2, 10), but not a *comprehensor*. His sufferings, bodily and spiritual, do not therefore require any special miracles. We are simply confronted with the one all-embracing miracle that God's Son is man and that this man is God's Son for us.

What Christ really rejected must therefore have been within

the compass of his earthly life. This is pictured in the hymn of Philippians 2 as "living at a divine level" (Phil. 2, 6f.); in Hebrews 12, 2 as "the joy that was set before him"; in the narrative of the temptations as using miraculous power to his own advantage and for his own spectacular public life. The gospels describe this in concrete terms as seeking that publicity that his relatives want him to pursue (John 7, 2-8), a publicity that finds its climax in the role of the Messiah-King which is offered him on several occasions. The offer comes mainly from the "freedom party", the zealots and their followers among the crowd, and such a role would then include action against Roman domination. The reality of Jesus' temptation is best understood when we reflect upon the fact that this role, in fact, stood open to him and that it appealed to him as a chance to establish God's kingdom. There is no need to think that Jesus refused this role because it was in itself sinful.

Although the history of the Davidic dynasty and of the descendants of the Maccabees showed the People of God how easily power can lead to sin, Jesus, on the contrary, could have played this part in justice and so have made the image of Emmanuel, in the literal sense, come true. Nor did Jesus refuse this part of a political messiah so that he could die on the cross for our sins: first of all, this role could also have led to his death on the cross, and, secondly, the death on the cross is not an aim which he pursued but a destiny which he accepted when it loomed up in front of him at the end of his career.

Our best approach to the secret of Jesus is to say that he refused the function of a political messiah because he felt himself called by the Father to be a prophet. For him it was a higher vocation to be the servant of Yahweh than to be the son of David or even Emmanuel, according to the letter of the prophecies. When Israel in exile cherished, as the ideal, the image of the Ebed Yahweh, the servant of Yahweh, it had reached a greater maturity through the Spirit than when it gave rise to the image of the theocratic Messiah. And this, firstly, because the image of human failure and suffering assumes here a positive significance (which it does not have even in the Book of Job), and secondly, because God finds a more direct approach to the human heart through the meekness of the prophet than through the power of the king, even when this king does justice to the poor.

It is precisely this supremely human way of the defenseless word, embodied in a whole person, which is stronger than any political power. The latter can force others to action, the former can convert the human heart. Now, it is through this conversion of the human heart that Jesus wanted to establish the kingdom of his Father. This seems to me the deepest reason why Jesus rejected a political kingship, however just.

Together with the rejection of power, Christ obviously rejected all lust for power and all abuse of power. What we count as "equality with God" he did not pursue as a trophy, but he emptied himself of power and right, and, as Robinson put it so strikingly, of all concentration upon himself.[9] He wanted to be nothing but the totally transparent mediator between the Father and his brothers: to give himself in this way was for him nourishment, life and self-affirmation. He was totally himself by being totally given over to God and the many, and if the consequence of this was the death on the cross, he accepted it and suffered it in the fullness of his love.

3. Having dealt with what Jesus rejected, it is hardly necessary to show what he accepted. All human life grows out of situations that are not chosen by ourselves but that we accept and make our own as we become more mature. It leads to some dominant choices and ends up again in accepting the situations that have arisen out of our choice and the consequent reactions. Jesus, as man, began his life in situations that were not of his own choice: within the human race invaded by sin, in a chosen people with all its history of salvation and calamity, in a Palestine dominated by the Romans and its own complicated religious and political relationships, in a Nazareth from which "no good could come" (John 1, 46), from these particular parents, within

[9] J. A. T. Robinson, *Honest to God* (SCM Press, 1963), p. 75.

the linguistic possibilities of Aramaic, with this particular environment to labor in, etc.

For Jesus, the "choice of his career" is that he does not continue the job of a carpenter in Nazareth but—suddenly or gradually—decides to lead the life of a preacher. By doing this he joins the existing career of the peripatetic rabbi. Within this framework Jesus makes a fresh choice and the most important one of his life: instead of political leadership he chooses the function of a defenseless prophet. In all this Jesus probably became only gradually clear about the circumstances of his life and the direction his life should take. At his baptism Jesus may not yet have seen that the painful end of the servant of Yahweh would be his.[10] Perhaps the fact that Jesus let himself be baptized by John shows that until then he considered himself a disciple of the baptizing prophet rather than a prophet in his own right. What happened immediately after his baptism must not be understood as an epiphany of the Christ to the crowd but rather as a theophany or divine experience for Jesus himself; as such, it implies that, from that moment, he recognized in himself the figure of the servant of Yahweh. Does he already foresee then that his death will have the significance of that vicarious sacrifice of atonement, described in Isaiah 53?

Against this it must be said that at the start of his preaching Jesus links the coming of God's kingdom only with the conversion of his hearers; that he begins to foretell his passion only after the hardening of the attitude of the Jewish leaders, and then only within the circle of his disciples (see, for instance, Matthew 16). Only when the opposition grows and opponents develop a truly deadly hatred of him does there dawn upon him the significance of the violent death that awaits him. Now he recognizes from the circumstances that his Father's will for him is to fulfill the function of the servant of Yahweh to the end, to

[10] This is presupposed by O. Cullmann, *Die Christologie des Neuen Testaments* (Tübingen, ²1958), pp. 65f.; English translation: *Christology of the New Testament* (Philadelphia: Westminster Press, 1964); this was correctly criticized by A. Vögtle, "Exegetische Erwägungen über das Wissen und Selbstbewusstsein Jesu," in *Gott in Welt. Festgabe für Karl Rahner* I (Freiburg, 1964), pp. 608-67, esp. 628-34.

die in order to bring the many to righteousness. Thus his horizon broadens out from the lost sheep of Israel to Jew and Gentile, and his mission develops from that of a prophet proclaiming salvation to that of the victim bringing salvation. This is what he chose and what he accepted instead of political messiahship. The task of rabbi and prophet was chosen, the death was accepted, or perhaps chosen insofar as he could have avoided it. In any case, however, acceptance is the most meaningful act he could make. It is the expression of his utter obedience and of his perfect sacrifice.

I have described Christ's *kenosis* from the point of view of the choice he made during his human life on earth; I have tried to answer the question of what he rejected and what he took upon himself. Now that we have reached the nadir of his death on the cross the term *kenosis* or "self-emptying" seems wholly justified: here equality with God is totally absent in Jesus. Even his human appearance is violated: "he had no form" (Is. 53, 2). We can understand why Ignatius of Loyola in his *Spiritual Exercises* makes us contemplate how in Jesus' passion "the divinity hides itself and lets humanity suffer most cruelly" (n. 196). Yet, closer reflection shows that the words *heauton ekenōsen* ("he emptied himself": Phil. 2, 7) should be understood rather in the absolute sense of "he made himself nothing" than in the relative sense of "he renounced . . ."

This is so, first, because what Jesus rejected was not a way of being or a possession but rather a possible future in his existence; and second, because the *einai isa Theō*, the equality with God, which "he did not count a thing to be grasped", does not refer to the real equality with God but our human representation and imagination of it. It is possible to understand it as what theologians want to ascribe to the incarnate Word, according to a somewhat mythical conception of the original condition of the first human beings and according to their idea of Jesus as *comprehensor*. But the divine condition that Christ did not wish to assume during his life on earth is rather what the informed or popular theology of his own contemporaries thought he ought to be: the glorious son of David, led by God from one victory to another. All this Jesus despised, but not the real equality with the Father, the unity with the Father, by which the Father was in him and he in the Father.

We may go even further and say that this true equality with God is not obscured but rather illuminated in Jesus' function as the meek, suffering servant who sacrifices himself for others. Conceived in this way, the *kenosis* of Christ did not obscure his divinity, but, through it, he revealed the divinity of both himself and the Father, "for God is love. In this the love of God was made manifest among us, that God sent his only Son into the world, so that we might live through him. In this is love, not that we loved God but that he loved us and sent his Son to be the expiation for our sins" (1 John, 4, 8-10). In these texts, as in the whole of Scripture, God meets us as love, not in the sense of a self-sufficient and self-centered love, but in that of a love toward us which surpasses all limitation. This love of "God-for-us" shows itself foremost in Jesus as the "Man-for-other-men" unto the death on the cross. Hence the crucified Christ is for Paul "God's power and God's wisdom" (1 Cor. 1, 24).

The utter "self-emptying" of Jesus shows itself in a love that maintains itself in the face of the death inflicted upon him, a love that deliberately endures this death for the sake of his enemies. "Greater love has no man than this, that a man lay down his life for his friends" (John 15, 13): this word is fulfilled in Jesus, and more than fulfilled in that he finds us his enemies and makes us his friends. "Why, one will hardly die for a righteous man— though perhaps for a good man one will dare even to die. But God shows his love for us in that while we were yet sinners Christ died for us" (Rom. 5, 7f.). Thus Christ's self-emptying, down to and including his death on the cross, preeminently reveals his equality and unity with the being of the Father who is love. It reveals at the same time his person and his humanity, because, while he fulfills the mission to bring the Father's love down to us in the obedience of the servant, he does it above all in the complete faith and total trust of the Son, even in the free-

dom of the Lord, so that for John Jesus is "exalted" on the cross
(John 3, 14; 8, 22-28; 12, 32f.). The more radical the self-
emptying, the fuller the outpouring of love toward us, but also
the more reckless the trust in the Father—a hope against all
hope that the Father's love will have the victory.

José María González-Ruiz/*Málaga, Spain*

Redemption and Resurrection

I

OLD TESTAMENT BACKGROUND TO SAINT PAUL

The purpose of this study is a limited one: to point out the essential links between the two great theological expressions, *redemption* and *resurrection,* as they occur throughout the New Testament. One cannot start with a definition of either term, simply because this definition will emerge from an analysis of the relationship that binds one to the other.

It is an obvious fact that Western theology has lost sight of the concept of resurrection to an alarming degree, and that this has led to a narrowing down of the notion of redemption, which has been virtually confined to the moral sphere, removed from the spatial and temporal context in which the history of humanity must inevitably unfold.

This eclipse of the idea of resurrection in the sphere of the theology of salvation has given rise to various mystical and ascetical spiritualities closer to the old Platonic tradition than to New Testament soteriology, which is firmly anchored in the bodily resurrection of Christ and the future resurrection of mankind.

The decline of the most essential "anastasian" element of the redemption of Christ has made Christianity appear a religion of evasion, set against worldly values and alien—if not hostile

—to the powerful ascending rhythm of the history of mankind.

The New Testament material covering these two terms is immense. I propose to concentrate on the great texts in which both realities—redemption and resurrection—appear as indissolubly linked in a dialectical relationship.

1. *The Pauline Texts that Present the Blood of Christ*
   as an Expiatory-Purgative Element and the "Giving
   up of Christ as an Expiatory Sacrifice—a True
   'Kippur' "—for the Remission of Sins

St. Paul, starting with the fact of Christ's redeeming death, develops his thought in a direct line, showing this death of Christ as an "expiatory sacrifice", within the framework of Jewish ritual. The texts that speak of the purifying power of Christ's blood (Rom. 3, 25; 5, 9; Eph. 1, 7; Col. 1, 20) all belong to this concept of expiatory sacrifice. Likewise, the passage in which Christ's death is spoken of as a sacrifice, Christ himself being the victim of the sacrifice, and the sacrifice bringing about the remission of sins, all belong to the same ideological context (Eph. 5, 2. 25. 26; 2 Tim. 2, 5-6; Tit. 2, 14; Gal. 2, 20; Gal. 1, 4; Rom. 8, 32).

This first series of texts shows clearly that Paul is thinking of the levitic rite of expiation through blood. The use of the Greek *hilasterion* which is generally used in the Septuagint to translate the Hebrew verb *kipper* puts us on the real track of his thought; in order to understand it properly it is necessary to point out what this term and the ideas of *kipper* and blood meant in the levitic ritual.[1]

The basic idea of ritual expiation, as expressed in the verb *kipper* is that of a specific, definite rite: the rite of the sacrifice of expiation or reparation, which wipes out sin and impurity to bring (or restore) persons and things into a particular state of being pleasing to God, united with the divine.

The basic text is in Leviticus 17, in which this cathartic use

[1] I have made extensive use of the magnificent and exhaustive work by L. Moraldi, *Espiazione sacrificale e riti espiatori nell' ambiente biblico e nell' Antico Testamento* (Rome, 1956).

of blood is specifically alluded to, and the reason given: "Because the life of the flesh is in the blood; and I have given it to you for the altar, to purify your lives, since blood purifies (ye kapper) inasmuch as it is life. . . ." (Lev. 17, 11; cf. Lev. 17, 10-14; Gen. 9, 4; Deut. 12, 13). So it is not a question of the material properties of blood, but of blood as a life-force: the term dāmō bnaphsō may be an apposition linked by an essential "b";[2] in any case nepheš and dam are intimately linked.

For the Semites, blood was the first element to be considered life-giving, the carrier and the principle of life. Then another concept gained ground, in which breath (nepheš) was seen as the life-principle. This can be seen in several Mesopotamian creation myths, and the biblical narrative itself. The two currents soon found a meeting point: blood is the life-principle, not in itself, but as the vehicle of the air element (nepheš) in life; in other words, the life-principle is the steam given off by hot blood. This purifying character of blood "inasmuch as it is life", is emphasized in priestly legislation by the declaration that all that has contact with the dead, with corpses, is impure (Num. 19, 11-12; 19, 2-10; Lev. 21, 11f.).

The place given to death by the men of the Old Testament is the underlying reason for these rituals. For them, as J. Pedersen says,[3] there was a sphere of death which broke into life. Anything that threatened life—the desert, the sea, sin, illness, chaos, darkness—is related to death, the present hostile reality that will one day be conquered. Like all the Semitic peoples, Israel professed belief in the fated and inevitable nature of death, classically expressed in these lines from the Epic of Gilgamesh: "When the gods made the human race, they gave death to the human race, but life they kept in their own hands." This theme of life belonging in full only to the divinity is illustrated in the Genesis parable of the tree of life. Man has never eaten the fruit of this tree; only when he had disobeyed the divine command by eating from the tree of knowledge is he forbidden access to the tree of

[2] P. Jouon, Grammaire hebraique, par. 133c.
[3] Israel, Its Life and Culture I-II (London and Copenhagen, 1926), p. 453.

life, and if he had not gone against the divine command, Yahweh
would have granted him the right to eat from the tree of life, but
as an extra grace added to his original human nature. By dis-
obeying, man has definitely cut himself off from this possibility:
because of this he will die, and so his death takes on the appearance of a punishment.[4]

Life, then, is a gift from God, a favor which he bestows, in its
fullness, on those who love him and obey him. This explains the
fact that in the Old Testament man is usually seen as receiving
his reward from God in his lifetime, and a long life is taken to
be the reward of the just. Hence, the confusion caused by the
early death of a just man. It seemed to cast doubt on divine
justice.

So gradually belief in a future resurrection, a revenge of the
"living God" on the "process of death" and *sheol* took shape in
Israelite thought (Num. 14, 28; 2 Kgs. 2, 2; Jer. 10, 10; Ezek.
10, 31; 33, 11). Two men stood out from earliest times as having been snatched from the empire of death: Enoch, who was
"taken up" as a reward for his piety, because he "walked with
God" (Gen. 5, 24) and the prophet Elijah, the prototype of
justice and integrity (2 Kgs. 2, 1-11). Yahweh, the "living
God", could not be limited by death in his life-giving creative
acts, and so from time to time he demonstrated his power to
bring the dead back to life. The Old Testament recounts three
cases of bringing back to life (1 Kgs. 17, 17ff.; 2 Kgs. 4, 29;
13, 21), all three cases of the dead being recalled to life by
Yahweh himself, acting through his instrument, the prophet
(1 Kgs. 17, 26). More familiar was the idea of the resurrection
of a people (Hos. 6, 1-12), and the two are combined in a most
significant way in Ezekiel 37 where what is at stake is not merely
the social renewal of a people, but the resurrection of the dead.
The question, "Will these bones live again? Lord, you know",
expresses a doubt which was never present in the clear case of
national resurgence. The dead are here called *ha nigîm*, those
who have been killed, and this view parallels what Daniel was

---

[4] E. Jacob, *Theology of the New Testament* (London, 1958).

later to call the martyrs, those who will be the first beneficiaries of the resurrection.[5] Equally, the idea in Ezekiel 34, 23 and 37, 24 of David come back to life seems to favor the concept of the resurrection of the king as a prelude to a general resurrection.

The scheme of death and resurrection appears in the figure of the servant of Yahweh, particularly in the admission of the people, "We thought that he was wounded by God. . . ." (Is. 53, 4). This resurrection of the servant is clearly presented as an extraordinary case which could happen to an individual only in the most exceptional circumstances. But, as E. Jacob has shrewdly observed,[6] all extraordinary divine interventions in the Old Testament—the gift of prophecy, the priesthood, any form of election—tend to pass from the particular to the universal. This happens in the case of resurrection: it gradually acquires a more general character as it comes to be seen as the only solution to the problem of retribution in the crises which this dogma went through in ever-increasing number. Resurrection as the solution to the problem of retribution finally became a definite dogma, as expressed in 2 Maccabees 7, 22 and in Daniel 12.

We are now in a better position to understand the significance of the rite of expiation by blood. Blood expiates or purifies by virtue of the life that is in it: when touched by "life" (blood), "death" (sin) disappears. The greatest positive element that God has placed in creation eliminates all negative elements built up by human frailty.

This does not mean, however, that the rite of expiation had a merely negative meaning: purification, the removal of sin-death. Its nature was essentially positive: blood does not only eliminate evil, but it reunites to the source of all good, or, more precisely, strengthens a weakened union with new life. This aspect of the rite coincides with the use and meaning of blood in the covenant, where blood, precisely because it is the vital element, was used as a symbol of union between the two parties, strengthening a mutual pact.

[5] *Ibid.*, p. 250.
[6] *Ibid.*, p. 251.

2. The Blood of Christ as a Purifying Element in St. Paul

Returning to St. Paul, and without going into a detailed exegesis for which there is no space here, we are left with the deposit of his insistent affirmations. Paul uses all the terminology of expiation by blood in the Jewish ritual and applies it to Christ.

The blood of Christ has the same significance as in the expiatory rites: first, negative—it wipes out sin (Rom. 3, 25; Eph. 1, 7); second, positive—it reunites those who were separated (Eph. 2, 13), restores the peace of the covenant (Col. 1, 20), and assures justification (Rom. 5, 4). This double value is the only one given to the blood of Christ in the first group of texts, those in which his blood is specifically mentioned.

In the second group of texts, those describing the death of Christ as a sacrifice, the same *single* effect of this sacrifice is *always* given: the negative-positive purification of those who believe (Gal. 1, 4; 2, 20; Rom. 8, 32; Eph. 5, 25f.; 1 Tim. 2, 5-6; Tit. 2, 14). So the redeeming, purifying, soteriological value of the death of Christ lies, for St. Paul, precisely in the fact that the blood of Christ is the bearer and bestower of life, indeed of the true and only life, which includes the two aspects "remission of sins" and "resurrection".

As we have noted, the purifying value of blood lay precisely in the *nepheš*, the vital breath of newly spilt, still warm blood. So an animal had to be sacrificed on each occasion, so that its warm, still living blood could be used in the process of catharsis. Coagulated, dried, cold blood, lacking the *nepheš*, was no longer the element of life and purification, but had passed over to the domain of death and corruption.

This perspective alone allows us to suppose that when St. Paul speaks of the permanent purifying value of the blood—the death —of Christ, he cannot be thinking of dead blood, of death sunk forever in the *sheol*, but, on the contrary, of warm, still living and life-bearing blood, of death overcome, reborn from its own ashes. To the Jewish mind, death itself could not be considered a life-giving element except insofar as it was a paradoxical negation of itself. *Death as death* could not be thought of as an element of purification and renovation, but *death as life* could.

II

CHRIST AS PRIEST AND VICTIM IN A HEAVENLY LITURGY

The conclusion we are attempting to draw from St. Paul's view of the sacrificial death of Christ is clearly expressed in later New Testament writings: the Epistle to the Hebrews, the writings of St. John and the Apocalypse.

1. *The Judaeo-Christian "Midrash" of the Epistle to the Hebrews*

The Epistle to the Hebrews has a double orientation: the thought of St. Paul and a Judaeo-Christian *midrash* of the priestly character of Christ and the sacrificial value of his death. This leads, as we shall see, to the specific affirmation that the blood of Christ has a permanent purifying value *because it is the blood of one risen from the dead.*

The writer shows the greatest interest in presenting Christ as the one true High Priest, and centers his midrashic evidence for this on the great pontifical rite of "Yom Kippur". The kernel of his argument is in the triumphal passage 9, 11-14: "But when Christ appeared as a high priest of the good things that have come, then through the greater and more perfect tent (not made with hands, that is, not of this creation) he entered once for all into the Holy Place, taking not the blood of goats and calves but his own blood, thus securing an eternal redemption. For if the sprinkling of defiled persons with the blood of goats and bulls and with the ashes of a heifer sanctifies for the purification of the flesh, how much more shall the blood of Christ, who through the eternal Spirit offered himself without blemish to God, purify your conscience from dead works to serve the living God?" The comparison is based on a sharp *a fortiori* contrast, between the lesser and the greater, type and anti-type.

First contrast: the great sanctuary in which Christ's expiatory sacrifice takes place is heaven itself, "for Christ has entered not into a sanctuary made with hands, a copy of the true one, but into heaven itself, now to appear in the presence of God on our behalf" (9, 24).

Second contrast: the priest used blood "not his own" (9, 28) in the rite of expiation; Christ uses "his own blood" (9, 12). And this antithesis is heightened by the fact that the "blood not his own" used by the Jewish priest was the blood of an animal (9, 13).

Third contrast: the Jewish priesthood had to be numerous because its members were mortal. Christ, on the contrary, "continues forever", he has risen, conquering death once and for all, and is consequently "able for all time to save those who draw near to God through him, since he always lives to make intercession for them" (7, 23-25).

Fourth contrast: the expiatory sacrifice required a *different victim* each time: in Christ's sacrifice, the victim, himself, is always the same (9, 25-28; 10, 11-17), because he is a living victim, "seated at the right hand of God" (10, 12).

To sum up: Christ's expiatory sacrifice is valid precisely through what is living and eternal in all its elements: a living priest triumphing over death; an ever-living victim, whose vital, warm blood has the power of everlasting purification; a permanent and definitive sanctuary, heaven itself.

So this interpretation makes the soteriological efficacy of the death—the blood—of Christ inseparable from the resurrection: Christ's bloody sacrifice has purifying value because it is the sacrifice of one risen from the dead.

2. *Johannine Writings*

John's christology would appear to unfold along the same lines. His writings are filled with his determination to find, in the smallest details of Christ's life and actions, reflections, sometimes hidden or latent, of the divine *doxa,* or glory.

In John Life Is the Resurrection: The figure of the risen Christ dominates his whole magnificent conception. One could say that his intention is to project the image of the resurrection behind every aspect of Jesus' life on earth.

From the beginning of John's gospel the resurrection is presented as the great "sign" of Jesus' messianic authority (2, 18-22). In Jesus' conversation with Nicodemus, in which his death is described as a "lifting-up" (3, 14), Jesus begins by describing his "ascension into heaven" (3, 13) as the true meaning and justification of his death-glorification; that is, a death which had not led us to a life "lifted up" could not be called a "lifting up". In the allegory of the good shepherd, Jesus talks of his death as the real distinguishing proof of the authenticity of his mission. At the end, however, so that his death should not be taken as a defeat—"a death as death"—he alludes clearly to his resurrection: "I lay down my life, that I may take it again. No one takes it from me, but I lay it down of my own accord. I have power to lay it down and I have power to take it again" (10, 17-18). To lay down life (*tithenai tēn psykēn*) is an expression peculiar to St. John (10, 11. 15. 17. 18; 13, 37. 38; 15, 13; 1 John 3, 16). It may correspond to the rabbinical "masar naphšô" (cf. "masar 'atsmô lᵉmitah"—"to give oneself, hand onself over to death"); more probably it is a variant of *didonai tēn psykēn,* intended to emphasize Jesus' freedom in choosing death;[7] that is, if Jesus had remained sunk in death without the possibility of taking his life up again, his death would have been a defeat, a victory of alien powers over him; it would not have been a death-exaltation. This it was solely because its outcome was the resurrection.

The same idea is expressed even more clearly, if possible, in 12, 23-24, where death is spoken of as "being glorified": "The hour has come for the Son of Man to be glorified." Then comes the allegory of the grain of wheat, again removing the possibility of a defeatist interpretation of his death: the grain dies, but not to sink and rot forever in the furrow; it dies to come to life again

[7] Cf. C. Barrett, *The Gospel according to St. John* (London, 1955), p. 311.

and bear abundant fruit. It is for just this reason that Jesus'
death is a "glorification": it is a step toward the fruitfulness of
life taken up again in the resurrection. This allegory of sowing
had also been used by St. Paul to illustrate the eschatological
resurrection (1 Cor. 15, 36-37. 42-44).

Finally, this viewpoint enables us to understand perfectly the
deliberate amalgamation that St. John makes (13; 14) of two
conversations that Jesus had on two different occasions: the
Last Supper on the eve of his passion and the farewell meal on
the day of his ascension (Acts 1, 4). John's concern is to present
an overall view of the death and glorification of Jesus, simply
because his death was not an end in itself, but a passage into
life, a departure "out of this world to the Father" (John 13, 1).

Of the greatest interest for our particular concern in this
article, however, is the speech on the Bread of Life in Chapter 6
of St. John's gospel. Jesus is the "Bread of Life" (6, 35. 48),
the "living bread" (6, 41. 51), precisely because he is capable of
raising those who eat it into eternal life, which is none other
than the resurrection (6, 39-40. 54). The Jews were doubly
scandalized by this statement—firstly (6, 41-43) because they
saw Jesus as a man of ordinary human stock and not of divine
origin as he was claiming. Secondly (6, 60-63), because it appeared to them offensive (*oklēros*) and insulting to their dignity
to receive sacrificial "purification" through the medium of
"flesh".

Jesus is in fact alluding clearly to his sacrificial death, to be
commemorated in the eucharist, as it is recorded by Luke and
Paul (Luke 22, 19; 1 Cor. 11, 24-26). The terminology he
employs is clearly that of sacrifice: the double meaning carried
by *didōmi* ("to hand out" and "to give over to death") is a
typically Johannine touch.[8] The preposition *hyper* with the
genitive has a sacrificial meaning throughout St. John, to "die
for" (10, 11. 15; 11, 50-52; 15, 13). It is used with a technical
sacrificial term, referring to Jesus' death, in 17, 19 (*hyper autōn*

---

[8] O. Cullmann, *Les Sacrements dans l'Evangile johannique* (Paris,
1951), p. 67.

ego hagiazo emauton: ". . . and for their sake I consecrate my-self").

The Jews clearly understood that Jesus was meaning to tell them that his "flesh", offered up in sacrifice through his death, was to have a permanent expiatory effect. To Israelite ears this was frankly incomprehensible and intolerable. John, as we have seen, has as his overall purpose to show the "kenotic" contrast between the "flesh" of Christ and the *doxa* projected over the humility and lowliness, temporal and physical, of that "flesh". Here again he takes care to overcome the lack of comprehension of his listeners (and readers): certainly "flesh" which is merely "flesh", immolated and sunk in the defeat of the tomb, cannot be an instrument of life. The sacrificial animal "purified" only through its "blood", still warm blood, endowed with the breath of life.

Jesus recognizes the difficulty, although he denies its basis: "Do you take offense at this? Then what if you were to see the Son of Man ascending to where he was before?" (6, 61-62). The same idea again: the sacrificed flesh of the Son of Man has been snatched from the defeat of death and restored to eternal life. In other words, he can speak of himself as being "glorified" in death simply because it will end in his resurrection and ascension. "It is the spirit that gives life, the flesh is of no avail" (6, 63). The true significance of this phrase can, I think, be grasped only in the exegetical context that we are examining.

The binomial "spirit-life" is very common in the Old Testament. God is the "giver of life" who infuses life into being, by means of the "breath of life" (*rûh, pneuma, pnoe;* Gen. 2, 7; 6, 3. 17; 7, 15, etc.). But I think John is here using a specifically Christian commonplace, already perfectly defined in 1 Cor. 15, 45: "The first Adam became a living being; the last Adam became a life-giving spirit." The contrast Paul intends is clear; Adam—"man"—transmits a physical life, which is transitory: Christ gives the certain hope of a permanent recapturing of life in the resurrection: "For as by a man came death, by a man has come also the resurrection of the dead. For as in Adam all die, so also in Christ shall all be made alive" (1 Cor. 15, 21-22). This "being made alive" clearly means, from the context, the eschatological resurrection. Adam was created in possession of a life which came to an end, and this is what he was able to pass on to his descendants, who were therefore transient beings, "from the earth" (1 Cor. 15, 47-49), "physical bodies" (1 Cor. 15, 44), in a word, pure "flesh and blood" (1 Cor. 15, 50).

Christ, on the other hand, even though he took the form of "flesh" is much more than that: he is a "life-giving spirit" (*pneuma zōopoioun*), a possessor of the divine breath that gives life. Seen like this, talk of a "Christ as flesh", sunk in the *sheol* and overcome by death, has no meaning. Christ as flesh (Christ-*psykē*) cannot be the new Adam; this has to be Christ-*pneuma*, made alive again and making alive again, or as St. Paul phrases it so well: "Christ . . . raised from the dead, the firstfruits of those who have fallen asleep" (1 Cor. 15, 20).

So there is a close link between the resurrection and the "life-giving spirit". Flesh and blood cannot inherit the kingdom of God; or, as St. Paul himself explains it: "the perishable (does not) inherit the imperishable" (1 Cor. 15, 50). "Flesh", unless it transcends its sphere of "flesh", is simply "corruption"; "flesh" in its mortal sense belongs to the enemy side, to death, "the last enemy" (1 Cor. 15, 26), and only when death has been destroyed can the final victory be proclaimed.

Turning back to John 6, 63, we find that the meaning of *zōopoiein* is "to make alive again". This verb only appears on one other occasion in St. John (5, 21) with clearly this meaning, as it is paralleled by *egerein tous nekrous*. Furthermore, throughout the whole of the Bread of Life speech, the life-giving power of the bread of life is emphasized (6, 40. 50. 52), that is, the life-giving power of the flesh and blood of the Son of Man (6, 55).

It is natural, then, that at the end of the 1st century, when Christian ears were accustomed to hearing the word "flesh" associated with corruption and death, and to considering the "spirit" as the only source of life, St. John should have tried to

resolve a difficulty that arose naturally from the cultural background of their situation. Jesus had actually said that his flesh
and blood, through his expiatory sacrifice, would become the
source of life and resurrection. How could "flesh" produce "life
and resurrection"? Jesus recognized the difficulty, but not the
thought behind it: that the *pneuma* alone can give life; that
"flesh" alone, unless it has been given life by the spirit, cannot
produce anything.

"The words that I have spoken to you are spirit and life."
John is not thinking now of Christ-flesh as the "Word of God"
(1, 1-14) or "Word of Life" (1 John 1, 1), but is referring to the
speech just made (*rēmata*), whose theme has been precisely the
binomial "spirit-life".

This, as we have seen, is John's overall purpose: to present
Christ as the Son of God, and to show even his earthly, "fleshly"
existence in this light. The "flesh" of Christ is something more
than flesh; it is the "life-giving spirit", it is the Son of God risen
from the dead and seated at the right hand of the Father, that is,
"glorified, raised up".

Now it is evident that the whole Bread of Life speech has an
underlying sacramental meaning[9] and a clear allusion to the permanent soteriological efficacy of the Meal as a commemoration
of "the Lord's death until he comes" (1 Cor. 4, 26). Accordingly, John underlines strongly the *doxa* of the sacrificial Christ.
This is no mere "flesh", sacrificial and sunk in everlasting death;
but flesh informed by the *doxa* of the resurrection, raised up to
eternal life and endowed with the "breath of life".

This same idea is expressed without allegory or typological
circumlocutions in 1 John: "The blood of Jesus his Son cleanses
us from all sin" (1, 3). This is not something that happened in
the past, only at the moment of Jesus' death on Calvary, but is
a present and permanent reality. So much so that he goes on to
affirm this presence and permanence of the "expiatory-purify-
ing" value of the blood of Christ in so many words: "If any one
does sin, we have an advocate with the Father, Jesus Christ the

[9] *Ibid.*, pp. 61ff.

righteous; and he is the expiation (*hilasmos*) for our sins, and not for ours only, but also for the sins of the whole world" (2, 1. 2). The parallel with the Epistle to the Hebrews is striking: here undoubtedly, as in Hebrews, Jesus is shown as High Priest and everlasting victim in the sanctuary of heaven, from where "he is able for all time to save those who draw near to God through him, since he always lives to make intercession for us" (Heb. 7, 25).

So St. John arrives at the same sacrificial conception of the death and resurrection of Christ that we have found running through St. Paul and the Judaeo-Christian *midrash* of the Epistle to the Hebrews:

1. Christ is the High Priest, who performs an expiatory sacrifice (*hilasmos* 1 John 2, 2).

2. He himself is the victim of the sacrifice, since the instrument of expiation is his own blood (1 John 1, 7).

3. The purpose of this expiatory sacrifice is purification alone (*katharei* 1 John 1, 7).

4. The object of this purification is a double one: (a) sin (1 John 1, 7; 2, 1-2); (b) death (John 6, 55. 64).

5. The soteriological efficacy of this sacrifice is not deduced from the negative aspect of "death", but from the positive side of the glorification of Jesus, now and forever alive as High and Eternal Priest.

To sum up, Christ the Priest, the redeemer of humanity, is precisely he who in the glory of his resurrection is constantly carrying out the process of "expiation-purification" by means of his living and everlasting blood.

3. *The Apocalypse*

This view of the glorious redeemer is already perfectly assimilated in the Apocalypse. In the writer's salutation Jesus Christ is presented as "the faithful witness, the first-born of the dead . . . who loves us and has freed us from our sins by his blood and has made us a kingdom, priests to God his Father" (Apoc. 1, 5-6).

In 1, 18 Jesus reveals himself as "the living one; I died and behold I am alive forevermore, and I have the keys of death and Hades". Jesus is "the living one", the essential property of him who calls himself "the living God", "he who lives", in many passages of both the Old and New Testaments (cf. Apoc. 10, 6; John 5, 26; 11, 25; 14, 6). "And it is precisely as 'the living one' that Christ has full power to raise himself up from the dead. He, of his own accord, has passed through death (an historical event, one moment in his existence); this provisional *happening* is opposed by a permanent, everlasting *being:* life, without limitation of any kind, life in God, as St. Paul says in Romans 6, 9-10. This personal victory over death endows him with absolute dominion over death, the last enemy of man (1 Cor. 15, 26), and over Hades, the personification of death" (Apoc. 6, 8; 20, 13-14).[10]

In Judaism, this possession of the keys of death and of the *sheol* was the exclusive property of God. God is he who brings the dead to life. He alone has the power to bring back to life, since he alone holds the keys to sepulchres for the resurrection of the dead, and he gives them to nobody. All the actions that produce resurrection are attributed to him. For a moment he gave the keys to Elijah, and so the prophet will have some part to play in the final resurrection.[11]

In Chapter 5 there is a splendid epiphany of the risen Lamb. Christ "has conquered" (5, 5); this gives him the right to open the scroll and see it, that is, to tell, read, reveal and realize the contents; besides being the mediator of the divine plans (Eph. 1, 3ff.), he is also the instrument of their execution. He "has conquered": the past tense indicates a particular moment in time. Wherever he is associated with the activity of God in heaven, he appears as the sacrificial Lamb, with two distinctive characteristics.

First, although living, he appears "as though slain" (5, 6); in

[10] J. Bonsirven, *L'Apocalypse de S. Jean.* Verbum Salutis XVI (Paris, 1951), pp. 100ff.

[11] Cf. rabbinical texts in J. Bonsirven, *Le Judäisme palistinien au temps de Jésus-Christ* (Paris, 1934), p. 483.

St. John's gospel the risen Christ displays his wounds (John 20, 27); in the Apocalypse (1, 18) he says of himself: "I died, and behold I am alive forevermore." The marks of death borne by the Lamb are something more than scars that can always be seen: they reveal the perpetuity of his sacrifice (Heb. 9, 14). Second, the Lamb is filled with life-giving forces: "seven eyes which are the seven spirits of God sent out into all the earth" (5, 6), that is, the sevenfold spirit of God which the Messiah will possess (Is. 11, 1-2).

The hymns to the Lamb that follow (5, 9-10. 12) speak deliberately of the "ransom" brought about by the fact that he "was slain" (*esphagēs*), making possible the libation of "blood" through which those who have been ransomed are purified from their sins and admitted to the divine covenant, becoming "a kingdom and priests to our God". This vision of the Lamb in glory corresponds to the view of the Priest in glory in the Epistle to the Hebrews, with one difference: in Hebrews the quality of Christ as Priest is emphasized, while in the Apocalypse Christ is shown primarily as victim. But both correspond in showing Priest and victim in a heavenly liturgy. The sacrifice itself is performed in the sanctuary of heaven: all the epiphanies of the Lamb are unfolded in a wonderful liturgical context, with hymns and incense.

III

THE BIOLOGICAL MEANING OF CHRISTIAN MORALITY

The whole of Christian morality is dominated by the concept of redemption. Therefore the whole direction and content of man's pursuit of salvation will be affected by the sense given to this process of redemption.

A "redemption" reduced simply to the moral sphere without incorporating this relationship with the final "biological" triumph of human existence, will inevitably fall into an attitude of introversion and evasion.

St. Paul states this most emphatically: if the whole fine structure of Christian morality lacked the guarantee of a final victory
over the death of the body, he would renounce it and practice a
conformist, Epicurean morality. I propose to take the most expressive texts only.

1 Cor. 15, 16-19. 30-32. 58

For St. Paul, as indeed throughout the Bible, faith is a vital
posture affecting the whole man, consisting essentially in accepting the divine gift of salvation in order to be able to realize
human nature in its fullness; for this reason the content of the
God-man dialogue must be the resurrection of Christ, as firstfruits and guarantee of the resurrection of the faithful. So, if
Christ has not risen, there can be no general resurrection, and
our faith is "futile". The pre-faith situation is one of sin, since
sin is an objective state, "for whatever does not proceed from
faith is sin" (Rom. 14, 23).

Without the resurrection "those who have fallen asleep in
Christ have perished", in an unrelenting death: the immediate
post-death situation is clearly considered one of non-salvation.
So, since the existence of the soul separated from the body cannot be called "life", we would have—if there were no resurrection—to limit Christian hope to this world. Such a "hope" strikes
St. Paul as pitiable and unacceptable.

Apostolic "spirituality" is likewise based on the hope of bodily
resurrection. Paul describes the practitioner of the apostolate as
one "who lives in a permanent state of risk". He himself has just
been through frightful struggles in his evangelizing efforts at
Ephesus, which nearly ended in his death. The apostle can face
all such dangers simply because he is buoyed up by his confidence in the resurrection; without this it would not be worth
risking his life: on the contrary, he should then try to get the
most out of life, following the Epicurean maxim: "Eat and
drink, for tomorrow we die."

The whole of chapter 15, which deals with the resurrection, is
rounded off with an exhortation to remain "steadfast" in Chris-

tian moral conduct in the sure hope of a final material victory: the resurrection of the body.

2 Cor. 4, 14. 16-18

"Verses 16-18, taken out of their context, could have been written by Philo (or any Platonist). Like him, St. Paul distinguishes between the invisible world, considered as perfect and lasting, and the visible; his antithesis between the two men, the outer and the inner, is also reminiscent of Hermetic terminology. But if the Apostle's overall doctrine is taken into account, we have to take these verses in an eschatological sense, a point of view that was unacceptable to either Platonists or Hermetics." [12]

Paul points out a continuous and growing tension between "our outer nature" and "our inner nature". This dialectic must be understood in the context of Pauline anthropology, which never divides man into "body" and "soul", but into "flesh" and "spirit". Flesh is the situation of man left to his own resources, with a certain emphasis on his religious estrangement from God. Here "our outer nature" more or less corresponds to the "flesh". "The destruction of the flesh" is in direct proportion to the "spirit (being) saved" (1 Cor. 5, 5). Inasmuch as man is a "dual" being, he is subject at once to the action of the "flesh", or "death", and to the action of the "spirit", or "life": "so you also must consider yourselves dead to sin and alive to God in Christ Jesus" (Rom. 6, 11).

So, then, the real action of the "spirit" on the Christian, even when, paradoxically, it appears destructive, has the other aspect of a progressive influence toward a "glorious" end. And this glorious end is naturally none other than the resurrection of the body, as is specifically stated in verse 14.

In St. Paul, "suffering" (*thlipsis*) is a constructive element: the Church is built on "sufferings": this conception is neither Buddhist nor Hellenic in character: it is simply the fact that the forces of evil cannot be overcome without a bloody struggle.

---

[12] J. Héring, *La second Epître aux Corinthiens* (Paris, 1958), p. 45.

What alone justifies the presence of suffering in Christian existence is its necessity in the gradual process of building up the Church in the human milieu. So suffering, apparently degrading man, has over and above this a basic influence on his inner being, it is "building him up" for his full and definitive existence —the final resurrection. These considerations can explain the paradoxical morality of the sufferings of the apostles (4, 8-10).

Philippians 3, 10-21

These verses deal with moral progress (*peripatountas—summimētai;* v. 17) seen as a race in a stadium. The prize for the winner is the resurrection of the body: the "sharing the sufferings of Christ" does indeed lead to a death, not a purely biological death, but a death in which we become like Christ, and the only reason for this association with the sufferings and death of Christ is none other than the goal of participation in the obverse of this "moral" aspect—the resurrection: "that if possible I may attain the resurrection from the dead". The Judaizers preached an introverted morality, reduced to the level of deciding which meals were pure and which impure, according to a complicated legal code; well could it be said of them that "their God is the belly". The "shame" (*aiskynē*) refers to the sexual organ.[13] Paul is using a cutting piece of irony: they "glory in" that part of the body called "shameful"; Paul uses a play on words in the Greek: the opposite of "to glory in" (*doxazesthai*) is "to be shamed" (*aiskynesthai*).

Galatians 6, 7-9

The moral behavior of the Christian will have an eschatological result. The man who has chosen to live in the proud solitude of the "flesh" cannot reap any crop other than "corruption". The context here is again eschatological—"divine judgment"—as in 1 Corinthians 15, 35-38, where the terms "to sow" (36-37) and "corruption" (*phthora*—42, 51. 53 and *phtharton*)

---

[13] Cf. the Septuagint: 1 Kgs. 20, 20; Neh. 3, 5; Is. 20, 4; Ezek. 16, 36-37; 22, 10; 23, 10, 18, 29; in the New Testament: Apoc. 3, 18.

also occur. "Corruption" clearly refers to physical death, and "incorruption" to the eschatological resurrection (v. 53).

St. Paul means that man's sinfulness (*kaukēsis*)—the remaining-in-the-flesh—does not only separate him morally from God, but leads him to an eschatological consequence of complete existential disaster: "corruption", "death forevermore", the total loss of all hope of "life". The Christian's morally good conduct, on the other hand, does not only make him pleasing to God, but biologically sets him on the path of his full existential maturation: "eternal life", the eschatological resurrection. The parallel with 1 Corinthians is even closer in the final phrase (v. 9). Here too Paul is insisting that the only thing that makes the high moral teaching of the Christians reasonable is its final result—the resurrection. So he emphasizes the theme of efficacy in terms similar to those of 1 Cor. 15, 58: human effort is not only extrinsically meritorious, meriting reward, but in itself, provided it has been raised up by incorporation in Christ (*en Kuriō*), produces results in terms of human fulfillment which totally justify the activities of man in his worldly and historical context.

Romans 8, 5-6. 12-13. 17-18

These verses also deal with moral progress (*peripatein*—to walk). The "ways of the body"—"body" meaning the whole man in his exterior and visible situation—here refer to the man-in-himself, inasmuch as he tries to *act* on his own account. The Christian rises above this manner of acting (*praxis*), and "the death warrant of sin in our nature", knowing that this course leads straight to death.

The "glory" to which this Christian moral behavior will lead is clearly the resurrection of the body, placed at the end of history and linked to a consummation or fullness of the whole of creation itself (19-22). In Genesis 1-3 man appears as the meaning given by God to his whole creative work, and as responsible for creation, which he has to bring to a happy term through working in it under the guidance of God. In verse 20 it appears that he who "has subjected" creation is God himself, who positively made man responsible for creation and so linked creation to the risk implied in man's free will. But this submission of creation to human destiny, decreed by God, is based on a "condition" (*epi elpidi*): the hope of future freedom. The metaphor, taken from the pains of the woman in labor (v. 22), indicates that the transcendent destiny God has planned for creation is not something discontinuous and prefabricated, but essentially linked to the evolutionary reality of a world carrying another world in its womb, another world that will not be totally different from this one, although its fullness will be far beyond that of this world.

PART II

BIBLIOGRAPHICAL
SURVEY

Engelbert Gutwenger, S.J./*Innsbruck, Austria*

The Problem of
Christ's Knowledge

The purpose of this article is to present a critical survey of the new efforts to clarify the problems connected with Christ's knowledge and consciousness. Since these studies can be properly understood only when seen against the background of current opinions in dogmatic theology, we should begin by looking at the problems created by these current opinions. The new investigations are an effort to cope with problems that I shall survey briefly.

I

CHRIST'S HUMAN CONSCIOUSNESS

When we look through the standard treatises on christology, confusing questions definitely arise. We get the impression that the image of Jesus during his life on earth is too exclusively derived from axiomatic principles and too little from what the gospels tell us. The reason for this is that since the Middle Ages dogmatic theology was dominated by that deductive way of thinking which was then considered the ideal. When medieval theologians looked at the inner life of Christ on earth, they began by positing a kind of principle of perfection from which they derived every kind of perfection as necessarily implied and therefore possible. And so they were led to make many definite assertions, either contradictory, or conflicting with the sober data of the gospels.

Let me point to the idea that during his whole life on earth Christ's soul fully enjoyed the beatific vision. Now, if we begin by saying that during his life on earth Christ's soul had already achieved that final beatific state as a fact, how can we still speak of a genuine freedom in Christ with regard to the divine mandate of his death? We shall be forced either to water down the obligation of this death or to develop a notion of freedom that is no longer human. And how can we maintain that Christ suffered abandonment by the Father and death in the very depths of his soul when this very soul was permeated in its depth by ineffable, heavenly joy? Even if these two ideas do not contradict each other logically, they are bound to do so psychologically; there is no point in using logical props to forestall psychological obstacles.

The attempt to divide the human soul of Christ into different regions in order to house contradictory spiritual experiences is also hardly acceptable. For consciousness is an undivided and homogeneous factor, at least insofar as a definite conscious experience necessarily excludes its opposite from the psychological point of view when it reaches a certain intensity. If we prefer to ignore this fact we run the risk of implying more than one *ego*.

When we consider that the patristic teaching of Christ's relative omniscience (Christ knew all things, past, present and future) was expanded by the Scholastics (who, not content with attributing knowledge of all reality to Christ as man, required that this knowledge was actual in every possible way), then we realize that here, too, there is a questionable division of Christ's consciousness. Today theologians limit the ways of knowledge in Christ's human soul to the beatific vision, infused knowledge and acquired knowledge, although there are certain differences in the development of this teaching according to the particular character of various schools of theology.

But, apart from all these differences in detail, this kind of theology still inclines toward a division of Christ's soul into various areas (many theologians talk of "levels"). The reason is easy to see. For if the soul, because of its objective vision of God, sees the whole of reality in the divine substance, we may rightly ask whether the infused knowledge, which transmits the same contents, is not ousted and made superfluous since it has no carefully marked-off area in the human consciousness.

Finally, one is still faced with the question of what use acquired knowledge may be since it cannot add anything to the contents already supplied by the beatific vision and infused knowledge. And so we are forced to mark off another area to make room for acquired knowledge. Yet we have to admit that this acquired knowledge of Christ is more clearly evidenced in the gospels than is the beatific vision, while the matter of infused knowledge finds no serious support in either the Scriptures or the Fathers. This insistence on various kinds of knowledge in Christ shows, in any case, a tendency to exclude various areas of consciousness; this implies a breakup of the unity of consciousness in Christ. When we do this, we should realize what it means: one human spirit sees the whole contents of reality twice over and at the same time through two different kinds of knowledge, while an excerpt from these already known contents is presented once again through a third kind of knowledge. If all these three kinds of knowledge have a genuine function and operate simultaneously, one is practically forced to admit that they are received in three different centers of consciousness.

But this is not yet the end of the problems. Apart from the difficult, speculative question of how the created spirit can read the whole of the past, the present and the future in the divine vision which has been granted to it, there are weighty declarations in the Scriptures which militate against this optimistic view of traditional theories about Christ's knowledge. Here I may refer to Luke 2, 52: "And Jesus advanced in wisdom . . . before God and man"; and to Mark 13, 32 (cf. Matt. 24, 36): "But of that day or hour no one knows, neither the angels in

heaven, nor the Son, but the Father only." When we consider
that during his life on earth Christ asked questions and expressed
his astonishment about certain facts—all pointing to a lack of
knowledge—traditional theories are left with the choice of either
explaining away the clear statements of the gospels or introducing still another area in Christ's consciousness where he does
not know everything, while he *does* know everything in the re-
maining areas. In view of the passages in the Scriptures about
Jesus' lack of knowledge the whole problem becomes so acute
that we are justified in saying that the solutions proffered so far
lead us down a blind alley; their very artificiality betrays doubt.

It has also become relevant to clarify how the ontological fact
of the hypostatic union affects the soul of Jesus. There is no
doubt in the faith of the Church that the first-person statements
of Christ in the gospels indicate a consciousness of his divine
sonship. Even at the level of historical criticism one is bound to
admit that the historical Jesus was aware that he could forgive
sins and was Lord of the Sabbath, which, in the contemporary
Jewish context cannot mean anything else than that he was conscious of possessing the plenitude of divine power. Seen in this
light his claims to divine sonship assume the character of "once-
for-all" validity. Even when the gospels are considered merely
as historical sources, one reaches the conclusion that the "I" of
the statements made by Jesus presupposes a divine character.
But how must we interpret theologically these facts of Jesus'
consciousness?

The question of how the human consciousness of Christ experienced the divine sonship was provoked by modern interest
in psychology. In Catholic circles the question was first discussed
by P. Galtier.[1] Ultimately it is a matter of whether the ontolo-

---

[1] P. Galtier, *L'Unité du Christ. Etre, Personne, Conscience,* (Paris,
²1939). Later Galtier changed his ideas about the kinds of "self", but I
cannot deal with that here. I refer to his article, "La conscience humaine
du Christ à propos de quelques publications récentes," in *Gregorianum*
32 (1951), pp. 525-68. Nor can I deal with the peculiar correction in the
encyclical *Sempiternus Rex* which appeared in *L'Osservatore Romano*
and was maintained until its official appearance in the *Acta Apostolicae
Sedis* 43 (1951).

gical fact of the hypostatic union is grasped directly as a conscious fact in the soul of Christ during his life on earth or
whether he becomes aware of it *via* an objective vision of God.
Galtier opted for the second alternative and primarily distinguished between a psychological self, a substantive self and a
metaphysical self.

This must be understood as follows: man is conscious only of
those acts in which a constant element is present, and this constant element is the psychological "I". But the constant presence
of this psychological "I" demands a foundation, and this is provided by the substantive "I". This substantive "I", however, is
identical with concrete human nature, which, in turn (and ex-
cepting Christ as a unique case), is always a person and by that
very fact implies the metaphysical "I". This last point does not
apply to Christ because in him we have to recognize a sharp
distinction between human nature and divine personality.

How, then, does Galtier assess the personal statements made
by Jesus, since these clearly refer to a divine person? And what
is the psychological and theological background of these statements? Galtier maintains that Christ's soul enjoyed an objective
vision of God. In this objective vision it sees that the *Logos* is
hypostatically united to Christ's human nature. In this light, and
only in this light, the "I" is elevated to the level where it expresses the whole Christ. To put it in a simplified way: for
Christ's soul the divine person with whom it is hypostatically
united is something that is "known", not something of which
it is "directly conscious" (*etwas Ge-wusztes, nicht etwas Be-
wusztes*).

This view explains also why Galtier must introduce a psychological and a substantive human "I" in Christ. For, the objective
knowledge is not formally a conscious experience of the self;
it is rather something that the self must receive.

But this is not the only reason why Galtier saw himself forced
to work out this view. He tried to ensure the psychological au-
tonomy of Christ's humanity. It did not seem right to him to
account for the structure of Christ's human consciousness by

deducing certain conclusions from pre-established Scholastic axioms. He tried rather to understand the soul of Christ by approaching it from the ordinary experience of human consciousness. This would do justice to the statement that Christ is truly man and takes the human spontaneity of the biblical Christ seriously. Galtier's basic attitude expresses an approach that no modern christology can afford to ignore.

Galtier provoked strong reactions from the Thomists. Nevertheless, this opposition shows no agreement in detail. P. Parente,[2] H. Diepen,[3] B. M. Xiberta,[4] and others defend opinions that contradict each other seriously. There is only consent on one point, and this is an important one: according to Thomistic teaching there is an immediate experience of the metaphysical personality in the human consciousness, a point of view that holds good also in christology and with which one can but agree. Insofar as ordinary human experience is concerned, we should remember that man's objective perception distinguishes him from all other beings and that in this clearly defined position of the self man experiences himself unthematically as a metaphysical person. The same experience is present when, in exercising his freedom, he makes a decision that concerns his whole being. And whenever man asserts something about his self, he touches his metaphysical self as subject.

[2] P. Parente, *L'Io di Cristo* (Brescia, ²1955); *idem,* "Unità ontologica e psicologica dell' Uomo-Dio," in *Euntes docete* 5 (1952), pp. 337-401.

[3] H. Diepen, "L'unique Seigneur Jésus-Christ," in *Revue Thomiste* 53 (1953), pp. 66ff.

[4] B. Xiberta, *El Yo de Jesucristo. Un conflicto entre dos Christologías* (Barcelona, 1954); *idem, Tractatus de Verbo incarnato* (Madrid, 1954). Xiberta's views are dealt with by the following: F. Lakner, "Eine neuantiochenische Christologie?" in *Zeitschrift für katholische Theologie* 77 (1955), pp. 220-3; M. Cuervo, "El Yo de Jesucristo," in *La Ciencia Tomista* 82 (1955), pp. 105-23; F. de P. Sola, "Una nueva explicación del Yo de Jesucristo," in *Estudios Eclesiásticos* 29 (1955), pp. 443-78; B. Lonergan, *De constitutione Christi ontologica et psychologica* (Rome, 1956), pp. 143-4; E. Gutwenger, *Bewusstsein und Wissen Christi* (Innsbruck, 1960), pp. 39-44.

II

CURRENT THEOLOGICAL OPINIONS

What I have said so far illustrates salient aspects of the problem of Christ's human consciousness. It should also be obvious what a dominant place Christ's human knowledge and perception hold in this context. But how can we cut the knot of these conflicting theological opinions so that we obtain an image of Christ that is less full of contradictions and more in harmony with the image given in the Scriptures?

In recent years there has been a promising development in this field. If I read the signs rightly, we are beginning to reach some decisive conclusions. A series of articles on this topic appeared during these years. If only a few names are mentioned in what follows, it is only because these authors have made an important contribution to a new understanding of christology. There is no point in dealing with every publication in detail because it would prevent us from seeing what is truly new and confuse the issue.[5]

[5] Bibliography for the period up to 1956 may be found in R. Haubst, "Probleme der jüngsten Christologie," in *Theologische Revue* 52 (1956), pp. 145-62. For the period 1956-59, see Gutwenger, *op. cit.* For the next two years, see K. Rahner, "Dogmatische Erwägungen über das Wissen und Selbstbewusztsein Christi," in *Trierer Theologische Zeitschrift* 71 (1962), pp. 65-8. To these should be added for the most recent years: P. De Haes, "De psycholgia Christi status quaestionis," *Coll. Mechl.* 45 (1960), pp. 366-70; J. Latour, *La vision béatifique du Christ* (Dissertation presented to the Institut Catholique of Paris in 1960); A. Michel, "Science, conscience, personne de Jésus-Christ," in *Ami du Clergé* 70 (1960), pp. 641-9 (bibliographical survey); C. Morali, *Aspetti metafisici e funzionali della conscienza umana di Cristo* (Roma, 1960); A. Perego, "Il problema dell'unità psicologica di Cristo," in *Enciclopedia Christologica* (Rome, 1960), pp. 510-35. J. Ezquerro, "Significados del 'Yo' (En torno al problema psicológico de Cristo)," in *Rev. Esp. Teol.* 21 (1961), pp. 325-8; H. de Lavalette, "Candide, théologien méconnu de la vision béatifique du Christ," in *Recherches de Science religieuse* 49 (1961), pp. 426-9; A. Nyssens, *La plénitude de vérité dans le Verbe incarné. Doctrine de S. Thomas d'Aquin* (Baudouinville, 1961); A. Perego, "Sull'unità psicologica di Cristo," in *Eph. Carm.* 12 (1961), pp. 105-15 (the author deals here with an article by P. de la Trinité, "A propos de la conscience du Christ. Un faux problème théologique,"

For several years Karl Rahner has voiced an opinion which had been publicized for some time, when he suggested that, in christology, we should distinguish between an immediate but not beatific vision of God and the beatific vision proper as it is enjoyed by the saints in heaven.[6] Although the immediate, non-beatific vision of God struck dogmatic theologians as a novelty, we should not forget that St. Thomas considered it in all probability as a genuine possibility. Indeed, he does not mention it in his christology; he postulates for Christ a beatific vision in the strict sense of the word. But if we look at his *Summa contra Gentiles* III, 50, we find that the second argument mentions explicitly that the separated human spirit, which sees the world as created by God, desires to see also the divine cause of this creation. This seems to imply that God can be seen as the original cause of the world, and that therefore the vision of God is not necessarily "beatific" in the supernatural sense of the word.

A more existential way of looking at things also prompts the idea that God can be seen under various aspects. According to the existential situation of the creature, God can be seen as demanding obedience, or as the wrathful judge, or as the founder of the world, or as he who gives himself in love. Not every one of these aspects of the divinity brings about the ultimate beatitude in the one who sees God in one of these ways. The following thought must also be kept in mind: if the state of final beati-

---

in *Eph. Carm.* 11, 1960, pp. 1-32); E. Schillebeeckx, "Het bewustzijnsleven van Christus," in *Tijdschrift voor Theologie* 1 (1961), pp. 227-51; L. Jammerone, *L'unità psicologica in Cristo* (Rome, 1962); C. de Pamplona, "El 'Assumptus Homo' y el 'Yo' humano de Cristo, a la luz de la doctrina de Escoto y de Basly," in *Est. Franc.* 63 (1962), pp. 161-94; A. Perego, "Interessante studio sull'unità psicologica di Cristo," in *Divus Thomas* 65 (1962), pp. 378-85; K. Rahner, *op. cit.,* pp. 65-83; A. Vögtle, "Exegetische Erwägungen über das Wissen und Selbstbewusztsein Jesu," in *Gott in Welt* (Freiburg i. Br., 1964), pp. 608-67.

    [6] K. Rahner, "Probleme der Christologie von heute," in *Das Konzil von Chalkedon* III. This article appeared also in Rahner's *Schriften zur Theologie* I (Einsiedeln, ⁵1961), pp. 169-222. English translation: *Theological Investigations,* Vol. 1: *God, Christ, Mary and Grace* (Helicon, 1961).

tude cannot be reconciled with genuine inner suffering, then Christ, while on earth, cannot be at the same time in a state of final beatitude and yet undergo that inner suffering to which the scriptures bear witness. These reflections should lead to the conclusion that Christ's freedom with regard to his death in obedience and his ability to suffer must be maintained as certain facts.

The next question, closely connected with the preceding one, is: How does the immediate vision of God work out in detail? Is it an element of consciousness in the strict sense of the word, so that the *Logos* is experienced as the personal support of this human nature at the very root of the human consciousness, or is the *Logos* seen and recognized as this personal support in an objective vision of God? Rahner looked for the answer in the hypostatic union.[7]

According to the Thomist metaphysical theory of knowledge, being and consciousness imply each other as two factors of the same reality. This means that, at the highest level of being, which is the spiritual level, the two in fact coincide, so that here we can say that being is consciousness, or that being is being-with-oneself. All creation is potentially subject to the power of the creator and can therefore be lifted by God to a higher level of existence (*potentia obedientialis*). In the hypostatic union the person of the *Logos* seizes upon the potentiality of human nature and actually assumes it; hence this union qualifies Christ's human existence ontologically. As such, this union must therefore affect his consciousness (*Da die hypostatische Union die Aktualisation der potentia obedientialis des radikalen Angenommenwerdenkönnens durch die Person des Logos und somit eine ontologische Bestimmtheit am menschlichen Sein Christi ist, muss sie als solche auch Bewusstseinsereignis werden*).

I do not wish to pretend that this argument is conclusive by itself. For such supernatural factors as sanctifying grace, the indwelling of the Spirit and other qualifications of human existence, which all imply a fulfillment of this basic potentiality in

[7] *Idem, op. cit.* (footnote 5), pp. 74-5.

actual fact, are not experienced in our consciousness. Rahner himself admits: "What has just been said is meant only as an indication of my meaning and of the approach to a solution; it does not mean that all this should not be investigated with far more penetration and precision." And so the a priori argument remains suspended in midair. Metaphysical axioms, based on a limited area of existence, frequently become questionable when transferred to the level of the supernatural.[8]

It is perhaps more convincing to proceed from the human experience of personal existence. As mentioned before, in the process of perception man turns everything into objects, which implies that he experiences himself as something whole and distinct from everything else. When he exercises his freedom he disposes of himself in a sovereign manner as a complete entity. Perception and exercise of freedom, therefore, give man the conscious experience of his personality, his metaphysical self. We have to accept that Christ possessed the same human perception and exercise of freedom. But this postulates that, because of the hypostatic union, his divine sonship is a basic factor in his human consciousness. Otherwise there would be a metaphysical defect whenever he perceived something or exercised his freedom, a defect which would be recognized as such in view of his objective vision of God, but would not be overcome thereby. In principle, therefore, Rahner seems to be on the right track.

Schillebeeckx tried to reach the same conclusion by approaching it from another point of view.[9] He starts from the fact that the *Logos* assumed a human nature and therefore also a human consciousness. If I understand him rightly he means that the *Logos* is also humanly conscious of himself, *i.e.*, is also in a human way "with himself". This is at least a powerful argument

---

[8] In another context Rahner has tried to explain that the supernatural enters as a factor into the conscious; cf. K. Rahner, "Bemerkungen zum Begriff der Offenbarung," in K. Rahner and J. Ratzinger, *Offenbarung und Überlieferung. Quaestiones disputatae* 25 (Freiburg i. Br., 1964), pp. 11-24.

[9] E. Schillebeeckx, "Het bewustzijnsleven van Christus," in *Tijdschrift voor Theologie* 1 (1961), pp. 241-3.

of convenience in support of a conscious presence of the *Logos* in the soul of Christ.

In the further development of his thesis there is perhaps room for a query. It strikes one that he does not allow for a center of activity in the human consciousness. His objection that the center of activity coincides and is identical with the center of the self is valid only insofar as ordinary human beings are concerned. But it does not apply to Christ since in his case human nature does not subsist (in the Scholastic sense) in itself but in the *Logos*. In spite of this the causality of human nature remains. And if actions spring from Christ's human spirit, then this human spirit is precisely conscious of the fact that it is the cause of these spiritual actions. Who can doubt that such actions as human perception, the exercise of freedom, the control and direction of attention and others originate in the human spirit of Christ? In this sense we are fully justified in saying that the human spirit of Christ is a center of activities. To concentrate on consciousness exclusively as such, seems to suggest that all causality of Christ's human actions must be attributed to the person of the *Logos*. In fact, Schillebeeckx argues as follows: the center of activity is identical with the center of the self; the center of the self in Christ is the *Logos;* therefore the *Logos* is also the center of activity. What has been said shows that the major of this syllogism does not hold here.

Schillebeeckx also tries to strengthen his case in other ways. He points to the Trinity where a too narrow concept of the unity of divine consciousness is made more supple insofar as the relationships within the Trinity demand for each divine person his own form of the one divine consciousness. These thoughts serve him to explain that the *Logos* has a particular slant of consciousness within the Trinity. To this feature of the *Logos* within the Trinity the hypostatic union adds a human consciousness. But Schillebeeckx emphasizes that there is no distinction between a psychological and an ontological self in Christ, but that both are absolutely identical. The *Logos* is a divine self, made man.

I do not quite see how these sharp and pregnant statements

of Schillebeeckx should be understood. It is not likely that he means that the *Logos* possesses a created consciousness in such a way that the *Logos* is not only the bearer of conscious human experience but also the immediate recipient. That would be possible only if the *Logos* were endowed with a special potentiality. And should we not then have to say—apart from the question of the *communicatio idiomatum*—that, for instance, the *Logos*, who is God, himself suffers? For the sake of clarity I might put the question in this way: does the suffering of Christ's humanity inflict pain on the divinity of the *Logos* or not? If the answer is in the affirmative, then we land ourselves in theological impossibilities; if the answer is negative, then the hypostatic function of the *Logos* consists in being the bearer of a psychologically autonomous human nature. This question is justified since we cannot introduce a distinction between *Logos* and divinity which would imply that the *Logos* can suffer as a person but not insofar as the divine nature is concerned.

If I have understood Schillebeeckx correctly and my doubts are justified, then it follows that it is better to approach the problem from the point of view of the human consciousness of Jesus, just as in general it is better to proceed from the known to the unknown than the other way around.

III

CRITIQUE AND EVALUATION

It was Rahner who, taking a decisive step forward, made the greatest impression. But it should be mentioned that previously Schillebeeckx had expressed essentially the same ideas,[10] although Rahner's systematic development seems clearer. Rahner makes the divine sonship a basic experiential fact in the soul of Christ. It is the subjective pole of the soul's consciousness, "the simple and straightforward 'being-with-itself', the necessary conscious realization of exactly this substantive unity with the person of the *Logos*—just this and nothing else".[11] From this basic realiza-

[10] Cf. Schillebeeckx, *op. cit.*
[11] K. Rahner, "Dogmatische Erwägungen . . . ," p. 76.

tion of the divine sonship Rahner then approaches the human knowledge of Jesus.

Next, Rahner points out that human consciousness has many dimensions: "It can be reflective and peripheral, simple or explicit, it can be objectively intelligible and it can be a transcendental and unreflective knowledge situated at the subjective pole of this consciousness; there is knowledge that is accepted and knowledge that is repressed, there are things that occur in the consciousness of the soul which are interpreted by reflection, there is a kind of objectless knowledge at a formal level within which a definitely grasped object finds its place. . . ." [12]

In a second preliminary observation Rahner rejects the Greek idea that knowledge is the measure of man without further qualification. It is precisely in the unfolding of man's freedom that a certain lack of knowledge becomes necessary. A decision presupposes a certain area of the unknown into which the deed can plunge forward. If man knew everything to the last detail, whether present or future, his freedom would be paralyzed. "A philosophy of the person, of the freedom of a finite creature, of history and decision shows easily that risk, the going out into the open, the trust in what cannot be foreseen, the hidden aspect of the beginning and the end, and therefore a definite lack of knowledge, are necessary and essential to the self-fulfillment of the person in the historical decision of his freedom. Freedom, to be possible at all, demands the wise acceptance of lack of determinacy and of its own dark origin." [13]

From these preliminary remarks Rahner proceeds to the kernel of the problem. He places the basic experiential fact of sonship at the subjective pole of Christ's consciousness as something that is not reflective and not thematic. Just as the basic experiential fact of man's spiritual being and of his freedom is carried through in all man's doings and supports all man's doings, so also is the divine sonship present in all Christ's doings. This basic fact can become the subject of reflection without, in

[12] *Ibid.*, pp. 69-70.
[13] *Ibid.*, p. 71.

effect, exhausting it. The immediate consciousness of the divine becomes thematic and reflective in Christ's encounter with the world. To interpret himself he uses the material with which the opinions, the language, the customs and the ideas of his environment and his age provide him. One can understand that in this way this thematic self-interpretation of Christ becomes a progressive, historical process. It also implies that much will remain unknown. "It is wholly legitimate that we should wish to study in what intellectual and historical climate this thematic process of consciousness developed with regard to the basic fact of Christ being God and man, of the divine immediacy and of his sonship; what kind of ideas the historical Jesus could use as already present in his religious environment in order to express slowly what he always knew of himself in the ground of his being." [14]

One may wonder whether this presentation of Christ's consciousness does not ignore the hard facts of patristic teaching about Christ's perfect knowledge. The answer is that the patristic and later the Scholastic conclusions in this field have no binding force. The historical research which led Rahner to attempt a new approach shows that this teaching about the perfect knowledge of Christ was marked by one-sided emphases, constant fluctuations, the application of axioms that lacked theological insight, the neglect of Christ's "not-knowing" and the taking for granted of the Greek idealistic view of knowledge.[15]

IV

CONCLUSION

Rahner's thought has an element of lasting validity, the more so since the new interest in the Bible and biblical theology has

---

[14] *Ibid.*, p. 80.

[15] J. Ternus, "Das Seelen- und Bewusztseinsleben Jesu," in *Das Konzil von Chalkedon* III, ed. A. Grillmeier and H. Bacht (1951-4), pp. 81-237; J. Latour, *La vision béatifique du Christ*, Gutwenger and Schillebeeckx (for all three see footnote 5).

made us more alert to what the gospels tell us. In the gospels we find a Christ whom the ideas of Rahner suit much better than the psychologically untenable propositions of the older dogmatic theology. The reason is that Rahner lets the Christ of the Bible speak for himself, and takes this as the norm for his study. This was forcefully pointed out by the biblical scholar, A. Vögtle, of Freiburg.[16]

It is well known that there is often a certain tension between dogmatic theologians and biblical scholars. Biblical scholars always complain that an objective study of the Scriptures shows nothing of what in christology is frequently put forward as a "theological certainty". Vögtle is a modern and, among Catholics, a rather critical biblical scholar. When, in an important article dealing with Rahner's thesis, he not only breathes a sigh of relief, but shows in detail how closely Rahner's view agrees with exegetical findings, one realizes what a positive contribution has been made by Rahner to our christology. Nor should it be forgotten that in speculative procedure overall verification in application is in itself a proof.

When we look at the gospels, we see how often Jesus mentions the eschatological idea that the end is near. In his missionary work Jesus addressed himself in principle to Israel. Only later on did he see the failure of his mission, and later still realize that he had to suffer and die. But even in his early prediction of his suffering, the thought of a death for atonement was not yet present. Here, too, there seems to have been a development in the understanding of his mission. Vögtle has worked out this view with much scientific display, using the *Formgeschichte* method, among others, and has contributed much other material in support.

Whoever has followed the development of christology during the last twenty years will have a strong impression that real progress has been made, and the speculative difficulties which beset christology in the past have been overcome.

[16] A. Vögtle, "Exegetische Erwägungen . . . ," (see footnote 5), pp. 608-67.

Helmut Riedlinger/*Freiburg, W. Germany*

The Universal Kingship of Christ

The thought of Christ's universal kingship raises some rather difficult questions. How can the event of Christ reach beyond our human world and affect the whole universe? As man, Christ is indeed one with God and the eternal Word, but how can he, as man, mean something for the whole universe and even occupy a dominant position in this universe? As cosmonauts circle the earth, as universal space is drawn within human experience, as we enter upon a truly cosmic age, to talk about the universal kingship of Jesus begins to sound somewhat like gnostic mythology, no longer acceptable.

Why and how can a man whose history was wholly played out on our petty planet attain dominion over the whole universe? This is not only contradicted by the immeasurable dimensions of the universe, but one wonders whether such a dominion has any meaning at all. If there are other beings, composed, like man, of body and soul, what meaning could Christ's dominion have for them, since he led his whole life outside the sphere in which they live? And if no such life exists outside this earth, what is the point of talking about universal dominion?

Are we not thinking merely in terms of a geocentric or heliocentric image of the world when we talk of the whole universe being subject to Christ in his glory? What can his humanity mean for the non-human dimensions of time and space in worlds that are totally separated from our human history?

At the end of his life, Reinhold Schneider, who endured
tyranny and war with so much faith and courage, was deeply
perturbed by these questions. In one of his last books he wrote:
"But—and this is the most cruel doubt—if we see the sign of
Christ in history, how can we see it in the universe? . . . Never
was there so massive a menace to the strength of the faith. And
it needs unheard-of courage to call upon this cosmos as a witness
to Jesus Christ." [1]

In one of his latest works, *Winter in Wien* (*Winter in Vienna*),
Schneider expressed his distress and perplexity about the riddle
of the cosmos: "For me revelation is a personal word addressed
to him who can believe, not a word addressed to the creature,
to space and to the stars . . . In the immeasurable darkness
of the cosmos there feebly glimmers just one star. That must
suffice; more has not been revealed." [2] For him revelation is
addressed only to man: "The Lord walked only the path of man,
the narrow path; like Socrates he sought only man, and gave a
possible answer to his existence; as for the riddle of the cosmos,
he passed it by." [3]

Schneider voiced a grave temptation against the faith in the
age of the cosmos: Are Christ and Christianity relevant to the
cosmos or is the whole event of Christ concerned only with the
narrow path of human history? Is there such a thing as a "cosmic", universal kingdom of Christ?

I

CHRIST'S KINGSHIP IN PAULINE THEOLOGY

By far the most significant answers to these questions are
found in the epistles of St. Paul. In 1 Corinthians 15, 28 Paul
said: "When all things are made subject to him, then the Son

[1] R. Schneider, *Verhüllter Tag* (Cologne/Olten, 41956), pp. 220-2.
Cf. M. Doerne, "Theologia tenebrarum. Zu Reinhold Schneiders Spät-
werk," in *Theologische Literaturzeitung* 86 (1961), pp. 401-4.

[2] *Idem, Winter in Wien* (Freiburg i. Br., 41959), p. 241.

[3] *Ibid.*, p. 132.

himself will also be made subject to him who subjected all things to him, that God may be all in all." The hymn which Paul incorporated in Philippians 2, 6-11 also says that "at the name of Jesus every knee should bend, of those in heaven, on earth and under the earth".

The most important texts on the cosmic kingdom of Jesus, however, are to be found in the epistles to the Ephesians and to the Colossians. In Ephesians 1, 9-10 he says: ". . . so that he may make known to us the mystery of his will according to his good pleasure. And this his good pleasure he purposed in him to be dispensed in the fullness of the times: to reestablish all things in Christ, both those in the heavens and those on the earth." The hymn of Colossians 1, 15-20, says still more explicitly: "He is the image of the invisible God, the firstborn of every creature. For in him were created all things in the heavens and on the earth, things visible and things invisible, whether Thrones, or Dominations, or Principalities, or Powers. All things have been created through and unto him, and he is before all creatures, and in him all things hold together. Again, he is the head of his body, the Church; he, who is the beginning, the firstborn from the dead, that in all things he may have the first place. For it has pleased God the Father that in him all his fullness should dwell, and that through him he should reconcile to himself all things, whether on the earth or in the heavens, making peace through the blood of his cross."

During recent years biblical scholars have been at pains to explain this universal dominion of Christ in terms of the modern age.[4] A basic question is whether, and how much, gnostic motives have influenced this presentation of the universal kingdom of Christ.

Bultmann and his school have tried for some time to trace such motives in St. Paul's letters, particularly in Ephesians and

[4] Some of the earlier studies are: E. Walter, *Christus und der Kosmos* (Stuttgart, 1948); B. Brinkmann, "Die kosmische Stellung des Gottmenschen in paulinischer Sicht," in *Wissenschaft und Weisheit* 13 (1950), pp. 6-33; L. Cerfaux, *Le Christ dans la théologie de Saint Paul* (Paris, 1951).

Colossians,[5] which would indicate the need to "demythologize" the "cosmic" aspect of christology considerably.

On the Catholic side, the biblical scholar Franz Mussner, of Trier, emphatically rejects a "gnostic" interpretation of Ephesians.[6] At first he was convinced that the material used in this letter of Paul could be understood only in the light of gnostic teaching, but, after a penetrating analysis of the text he came to the opposite conclusion: the texts are quite intelligible by themselves, and there is therefore no ground for recourse to gnostic influences; the gnostic concept of a "cosmic" Christ who fills the universe cannot be found in the letter to the Ephesians.

Evangelical theologians, too, have recently made efforts to reestablish the independent character and inner unity of this aspect of christology in Ephesians and Colossians with regard to gnosticism. This will at the same time take Protestant christology out of its centuries-old anthropocentrism. It is noteworthy that in 1961 at New Delhi the representatives of the young Afro-Asian Churches objected that European Protestantism had neglected the cosmic dimension of Christ for centuries. It appears that Christians beyond the pale of Western technological society still experience a certain original closeness to this cosmic christology, an experience which proves almost impossible for a modern technical-minded society.

The Dutch Reformed theologian, Isak J. du Plessis, has shown a new interest in this problem in his dissertation on cosmic christology in Ephesians and Colossians.[7] He emphasizes the originality of Christian thought with regard to gnosticism: Christ is indeed the head of the universe, but he is not a "cosmic" man

[5] R. Bultmann, *Theology of the New Testament,* 2 Vols. (SCM, London, 1965), 1, pp. 164-85; H. Schlier, *Christus und die Kirche im Epheserbrief* (Tübingen, 1930); E. Käsemann, *Leib und Leib Christi* (Tübingen, 1933).

[6] F. Mussner, *Christus, das All und die Kirche* (Trier, 1955).

[7] I. du Plessis, *Christus als Hoofd van Kerk en Kosmos* (Theologische Academie, Groningen, 1962), under the auspices of the Johannes Calvijn Stichting.

whose corporality embraces the whole universe. Only the Church is the body of Christ, not the universe.

On the other hand, in his new commentary on the Ephesians Hans Conzelmann points again to the influence of gnostic images.[8] According to him the teaching of the recapitulation of all in Christ (Eph. 1, 10) goes back to the gnostic myth of the original man (*Urmensch*) who is identical with the universe, whose limbs are dispersed and are again brought together by him. In this way the universe is renewed and constitutes again the "body" under the "head", as it was in the beginning. This original man is therefore the beginning and the redeemer of the universe. Yet, even Conzelmann admits that, although this recapitulation of all in Christ is inspired by gnosticism, it has been given a new meaning. It is no longer part of a cosmology but should make us understand our new relation to God, revealed in history, as well as the new dimension of our existence. If I understand Conzelmann correctly, it is not ultimately a matter of how the cosmos is composed, but rather of extending to the whole universe Christ's relation to our existence. It is not a question of cosmic influences or of a universal power actually exercised by the risen Christ, but rather of interpreting our own life in the faith within the omnipresence and omnipotence of Christ.

Yet, the question remains what this universal kingship of Christ can mean in concrete reality. What kind of reality? Is it only the reality of the all-embracing, transcendent power of Christ the Lord as we see it in our faith? But is there any meaning in such a power of Christ which is totally beyond human experience? Should the cosmological interpretation lead over into one that is anthropocentric and existential? Or is it not rather a question of trying to rediscover the cosmic aspect of christology and of bringing it into harmony with our consciousness of the universe today?

[8] H. Conzelmann, *Der Brief an die Epheser,* in the series: Das Neue Testament Deutsch 8 (Göttingen, 1962), p. 61.

Heinrich Schlier, the biblical scholar of Bonn, who became a Catholic after having been a disciple of Bultmann, has recently made an important contribution to this question. He fully realizes "how far from and how alien to the modern mind are matters of faith which we think we know and which we consider so obvious.[9] He, therefore, stresses first of all that the origin of Christ's kingship lies in the will of God. "The kingship of Christ is not the fruit of human design and human will; it is not the result of historical or physical power. Its reason lies beyond all that is in heaven and on earth; it lies in God." [10]

This means above all that Christ's kingship cannot be approached from an anthropocentric or cosmocentric point of view. Understanding must begin with theology and ontology. This implies that we must not look on Christ's power as something "extra", something introduced from outside into a universe alien to Christ. From the beginning of creation the universe is geared to Christ in all its dimensions, bears in its very being the stamp of Christ, however much it may be hidden, so that the power of the risen Christ simply manifests the original christological structure of the universe, and shows it forth as operative. However much this power of Christ may cause the subjection and destruction of rebel powers and dominions,[11] its true nature is the revelation of Christ's mystery in the cosmos.

In the widely appreciated commentary on the Ephesians on which he spent many years of research, Schlier carefully explains the "recapitulation" through which the universe was given Christ as its head.[12] Contrary to the opinion of many Evangelical scholars, Schlier holds that Ephesians is a late work of Paul in spite of its peculiar terminology. On the other hand, he admits that there are gnostic influences in its language and imagery, which does not mean that Paul became a gnostic in his later years. Such gnostic elements as are incorporated have been

[9] H. Schlier, "Über die Herrschaft Christi," in *Geist und Leben* 30 (1957), p. 246.

[10] *Ibid.*

[11] *Idem, Mächte und Gewalten im Neuen Testament. Quaestiones disputatae* 3 (Freiburg i. Br., 1958), pp. 37-49.

[12] *Idem, Der Brief an die Epheser* (Düsseldorf, [4]1963), pp. 61-6.

wholly transformed by Paul into authentic Christian thought.

Thus "recapitulation", too, now has a genuinely Christian meaning. As the head, Christ truly embraces and builds up the universe. Its final cohesion and inner unity must be attained in him. And this implies that, in this way, it is restored to its original nature and its true purpose. The place where this recapitulation of the universe is already recognized, and where this headship of Christ already operates, is the Church. It is in and through the Church that the hidden restoration of the universe in Christ is revealed and transmitted to the world of man. God's will to bring about this restoration to such a cosmic extent remains a mystery beyond our comprehension. As such it does not occur in the human sphere, human tradition, human thought, poetry or action. But at present it has become manifest in the Church. Even so, it can be experienced only in a history of progressive fulfillment.

Apart from the historical event of salvation in Christ and the Church this "Christianization" of the universe is beyond the grasp of theoretical investigation. And so Christ's "headship" in the Church and in the cosmos is one and the same. The one cannot come about without the other or be understood without the other.

It is difficult to find anywhere such a mature and penetrating explanation of the cosmic christology of Ephesians as in Schlier's commentary. Unfortunately, there is nothing of such quality (at least among Catholic authors) where Colossians is concerned.

This letter has particular significance here because of the hymn (Col. 1, 15-20), which I have already mentioned. R. Bultmann and Ernst Käsemann assume that it is modelled on a pre-Christian hymn about revelation composed in a Jewish gnostic milieu.[13] On the other hand, Harald Hegermann has recently adduced serious reasons for maintaining the Christian origin of the hymn and for excluding gnostic influences.[14] H. Conzelmann,

[13] E. Käsemann, "Eine urchristliche Taufliturgie?" in *Festgabe R. Bultmann* (Stuttgart, 1949), pp. 133-48.
[14] H. Hegermann, *Die Vorstellung vom Schöpfungsmittler im hellenistischen Judentum und Urchristentum* (Berlin, 1961). S. Lyonnet

too, considers it a genuine Christian hymn in his recent commentary on Colossians. But he thinks that "it shows a Jewish mentality, already influenced by gnostic elements".[15]

Remarkable in this hymn about Christ is the expression "firstborn of all creation". It had already created difficulties for the Fathers in their conflict with the Arians, since it applied fully neither to Christ's divinity nor to his humanity. In the end, the application to Christ's divinity prevailed, which, nonetheless, demanded the tendentious interpretation of the phrase by translating it as "the firstborn *before* all creation".[16] But the poet obviously did not think of a distinction between divinity and humanity in the sense of the later doctrine about the two natures, but simply thought of the preexisting Christ as having an absolute primacy over all the rest of creation from the very beginning. He exists not merely before all things (1, 17) but participates in the creation of all things as mediator. In him, through him and for him (1, 16) all things have been created.

Conzelmann has pointed out that these triple formulae in this kind of style originate from the Stoa and are due to the pantheistic interpretation of the divine oneness, physical nature and humanity. In Colossians, however, this threefold formula was meant to assert the unification of the whole universe in Christ over against any dualistic separation of God and the world. When, after Christ is called the head of the body, the words "of the Church" are added, Conzelmann interprets this as showing that in the original composition it was the cosmos that was seen as the body of Christ and that the restriction of the phrase to the Church was an afterthought. According to him, therefore, the background of this hymn, as in the case of the hymn of

---

also prefers Jewish to gnostic influences; cf. "L'hymne christologique de l'épître aux Colossiens et la fête juive du Nouvel An," in *Recherches de Science religieuse* 48 (1960), pp. 93-100.

[15] H. Conzelmann, *Der Brief an die Kolosser,* in the series *Das Neue Testament Deutsch* 8 (Göttingen, 1962), pp. 136-9.

[16] Cf. B. Brinkmann, "Die kosmische Stellung des Gottmenschen," in *Wissenschaft und Weisheit* 13 (1950), pp. 11-2; J. Bonnefoy, *La primauté du Christ* (Rome, 1959), pp. 166-203.

Ephesians, was provided by a mythical cosmology which can be traced as far as Iran and India, namely, the world as the body of the "original" man.

But in Colossians the mythical matter is not used for some teaching about cosmology but rather in order to show that revealed salvation extends beyond time and space. The cosmic triumph of Christ is experienced in the Church as the deliverance from powers and dominions, as the victory over fear. The use of these cosmological references should also show that the place of this revelation is not a mythical "beyond", but the world.

At this point Conzelmann tackles the question whether, and how far, these cosmological formulae of the New Testament can still be used today. He rejects a mere repetition. In the field of cosmology and metaphysics these texts have nothing to contribute. Speculations of this kind would have been attempted precisely by those whom the letter sought to combat. The question is therefore how these cosmological statements can be made actual in modern preaching. How can we see Christ today as Lord of the cosmos? It does not mean "to provide a theory about cosmic powers, forms and dimensions but to give me an understanding of myself as created and redeemed so that I can understand my true possibilities in the world in the freedom of the faith".

Yet, does such a view not spring from a deep-rooted aversion to cosmology and metaphysics, and does it not restrict the meaning in a too anthropological and even subjective sense? It is true that we are not here concerned with metaphysical or cosmological theories, or with a view of a world without salvation and without its sacred aspect. But why should all this concern only "me"—"my" possibilities and "my" freedom? The perspective opened up by Colossians is much wider, embracing the whole universe with all it contains in heaven and on earth, the visible and the invisible, powers and dominions, and above all the community of the faithful, the Church. All these transcends "me" and "mine". Should modern subjectivism (individualism) so dominate the process of demythologization that, after eliminating the ostensible elements of gnosticism, there remains only what suits the narrow religious individualism of modern Western Christianity?

It seems to me that Conzelmann underrates the ecclesiological, cosmological and ontological dimensions of the incarnation. If the incarnation itself is not an element of gnostic mythology, but an authentic, historical event, then it must affect the whole nature of the universe in its very depths. The cosmos can then no longer be presented as forever abiding in its own cosmic existence. Nor can we credit the cosmos with a future independent of the event of salvation. In this case we would limit the incarnation to a purely anthropological event, preventing it from having any effect upon the universe. But this discussion takes us out of the realm of exegesis and into the systematic explanation of the problem.

II

Christ's Kingship in Dogmatic Theology

In the systematic treatment of the cosmic aspect of christology we seem to discover the same tendencies already noticed in the exegetical treatment. If I understand the situation rightly, biblical scholars tend either to treat the cosmic dimensions of Christ's dominion as more or less real, or to demythologize in one way or another the assumed gnostic material. In the same way attempts are made in the systematic field at a far-reaching union of christology and cosmology while on the other side of the fence there is a constant fear of mystification and "gnostic" confusion.

Manuals of dogmatic theology hardly bother about the problem which the cosmic dimension of Christ's kingship constitutes for modern thinking. They limit themselves to unexplained repetitions of the teaching of St. Paul. For the rest, one may say in general that Christ's primacy over the universe has for long been treated in a most inadequate fashion. In an excellent study

of the primacy of Christ in modern theology, Jean-François
Bonnefoy (d. 1958), an outstanding scholar in this field, expressed regret that theologians have paid so little attention to
this basic tenet of the Christian faith.[17] During thirty years of
research he found no development of this point in the medieval
Summae, the commentaries on the *Sentences* or in the collections
of *Quaestiones.* The point has been equally neglected in the
Enchiridion Patristicum of Rouët de Journel and the *Enchiridion
Symbolorum* of Denzinger. In many of the best theological hand-
books the problem is not even mentioned.

Yet, he found a great deal about it in the scriptural commentaries of the Fathers. And I may add that this holds also
for much of the medieval interpretation of the Scriptures, now
largely forgotten. Bonnefoy attributes this neglect to the fact that
there was too much discussion about the so-called motive of the
incarnation, and this on a purely hypothetical level. For, if the
question whether the Word would have become man if Adam
had not sinned was answered in the negative, as was usually the
case in Thomism, then the question of Christ's universal primacy
was practically blocked from the start. A view which concen-
trated too heavily on the anthropological aspect of Adam's sin
was bound to look in the wrong direction.

On the other hand, it cannot be denied—Bonnefoy proved
it—that the so-called Scotist approach is more acceptable since
it is based on the hymn of Colossians 1, 15-20 and so attributes
an unqualified primacy to Christ's humanity in the whole of
creation. This more scriptural approach seems even to gain
ground among Thomists. A prominent Thomist like the French
Dominican, Humbert Bouëssé was not afraid of adapting the
traditional Scotist view to Thomism and even to attribute it to St.
Thomas himself.[18] Thus the Scotists were able to strengthen their
position in recent times with greater confidence.

Among Franciscan theologians, the Italian, A. Sanna, pro-

---

[17] *Idem,* "Il primato di Cristo nella teologia contemporanea," in *Prob-
lemi e orientamenti di teologia dommatica* (Milan, 1957), pp. 123-235.

[18] H. Bouëssé, *Le Sauveur du Monde. I: La place du Christ dans le plan
de Dieu* (Chambéry-Leysse, 1951).

duced in 1951 an excellent contribution to the historical aspect of this view in his book on the Kingship of Christ.[19] Shortly before his death Bonnefoy finished his important work on Christ's primacy in Scripture and Tradition, in which he brought together what he had gleaned during many years of research.[20] He comments extensively on all the texts in the wisdom literature, the Ephesians and Colossians, which refer to this primacy. Unfortunately, the problems thrown up by the more recent exegesis of the gospels, particularly in Bultmann's school, are not dealt with, in spite of the scope of his treatment. It does, however, contain many interesting texts from the Fathers. On the other hand, the medieval and more modern tradition receives only sporadic mention. The systematic section attempts to explain how the universal primacy of Christ comes about on the basis of Aristotelian causality. What he says about Christ as the final, exemplary and efficient cause is no doubt most useful. But one may ask whether these causal categories are really adequate in this case and whether theology cannot, or indeed must not, approach the question of Christ's headship in a more original way from the ontological angle.

This decidedly Scotist approach of Bonnefoy's provoked criticism from the Thomists. Thus V. Boublik, of the University of the Lateran, pointed out that the Scotists limited the soteriological aspect of the question too much and stated that not just the incarnation, but the event of Christ as a whole was the center of history.[21] These subtle controversies between Thomists and Scotists about Christ's primacy are very important for the theology of Christ's cosmic dominion because they deal with basic issues. One can also agree that the approach to the cosmic christology of the later epistles of St. Paul is more easily made from the Scotist point of view than from the Thomist. Yet, all

[19] A. Sanna, *La regalità di Cristo secondo la Scuola Francescana* (Oristano, 1951).

[20] J. Bonnefoy, *La primauté du Christ selon l'écriture et la tradition* (Rome, 1959).

[21] V. Boublik, "Il primato universale di Cristo Redentore," in *Divus Thomas Piac.* 64 (1961), pp. 193-212.

these controversies do not touch the specific problem created in christology by the modern concept of the cosmos.[22] For scholastic theology has no little difficulty in tackling this problem, which arises from a hardly articulate basic attitude in modern man, with its traditional armory.

It now appears that an answer must be sought outside the process of scholastic theology. Thus there are observations which aim at a future convergence of cosmology, anthropology and christology in the recently published book by Emile Mersch, S.J. (d. 1940), on Christ, man and the universe.[23] Mersch does not yet aim here at a strictly conceptual formulation, but rather at an intuitive, mystical approach to the unity which Christ brought about between cosmos and man. He points to the cosmic dimension of the human spirit which is essentially related to the universe as a whole. He also shows how the immanent spirit of the cosmos is related to man in whom it becomes fully conscious. Thus the whole universe is human in its inner reality, while man is cosmic in his inner reality. The future holds hope for an increasing unity of man with the universe and, through the mediation of the God-Man, with God himself. This vision of the future development of mankind, which Mersch himself describes as "natural eschatology",[24] seems to tend, with far more determination, in the same direction as that chosen by his confrère Pierre Teilhard de Chardin (d. 1955).

Teilhard's theological intuitions clearly lie outside the scholastic tradition. They are still far from having the thoroughness, coordination and integration in the whole of theology which are required to give them theological authority. It is therefore not difficult to point to a certain inconsistency and incoherence in the ideas of this brilliant outsider who had little time for professional theologians and philosophers. But that is hardly all. In spite of all the legitimate and necessary criticism of Teilhard's

[22] H. Bouëssé, *Un seul Chef ou Jésus-Christ Chef de l'univers et Tête des Saints* (Paris, 1950) is more a devotional work and does not deal with the problem of Christ and the universe as it stands today.

[23] E. Mersch, *Le Christ, l'Homme et l'Univers* (Bruges, 1962).

[24] *Ibid.*, p. 87.

ideas, one has to admit that he tackled the problem of a cosmic christology and tried to solve it in a way which appealed to our modern cosmic age, and with an intensity which is beyond compare. As one who for many years gave of his best to the exploration of the origin of both the universe and man, he was more qualified than any other Christian thinker to attempt the construction of a genuine, cosmic christology. He was well acquainted with the scriptural basis contained in Ephesians and Colossians. But he could not rest satisfied with a sterile repetition of phrases, nor with a demythologization or liquidation of Christ's cosmic dominion. So the only thing he could do was to launch into unknown territory.

In 1916 he saw Christ in the material world in three ecstatic experiences. He saw the heart of Christ expand before his eyes and take on the dimensions of the universe. A sacred host expanded itself to all things, gathered all things in itself and, filled with all things, contracted itself again. Lastly, once when he received communion he tried to become one with the sacred host, but suddenly found that the universe stood between him and the Lord, and he had to pass through the universe to reach the Lord.[25] Since those events he felt himself called to be the evangelist of the cosmic Christ. In 1923 he vowed to live and to die in the body of Christ which is the universe.[26] Time and again the vision of the cosmic Christ occurs in Teilhard's writings, this Christ who is not a foreign Lord holding sway over his kingdom, but one who penetrates into the very depths of the universe, who urges on the process of cosmic evolution from within and guides it, so that, somewhat like the original man of gnosticism, the universe appears as his body.

Such a view inevitably provoked lively controversies which are still increasing. Some see in it the long-awaited synthesis of christology and cosmology brought within reach at last. Others

---

[25] P. Teilhard de Chardin, *Hymne de l'Univers* (Paris, 1961), pp. 39-58 ("Le Christ dans la matière"). English edition: *Hymn of the Universe* (Harper, 1965).
[26] *Ibid.*, p. 37.

suspect a blatant case of gnosticism, syncretism and perversion of genuine Christianity.

What is most necessary in this fierce debate is a cool and cautious analysis of Teilhard's real christological motives. It may very well be that, basically, he has something to say that may help us further in the question of cosmic christology, in spite of an unsatisfactory formulation that leads to misunderstanding. He was aware of the cosmic dimension in which modern scientific thought is so deeply involved because of his long life as a scientific explorer. His concern to extend christology to this dimension and to introduce this dimension into christology was altogether justified. One must even admit that the issue is so urgent today that anyone working in this direction deserves goodwill and understanding.

In Germany, the Redemptorist Alois Guggenberger tried to present Teilhard's christology in a mature and comprehensible manner.[27] He did not believe that Teilhard could be accused of a naturalistic or gnostic solution of the mystery of Christ: "Teilhard maintained the supernatural character of Christ's mystery in its integrity."[28] Indeed, he indicated that Teilhard was most concerned to maintain a personal being at the highest peak of the world's evolution in its fulfillment. Without such a fulfillment, which only a God-Man can bring about in reality—because as man he belongs to the cosmos and as God he reaches the greatest height of personalization—his universe would seem to him only half personalized. Thus there is actually within the cosmos a tendency, which cannot be resisted and which can be recognized by the scientist, toward supreme personalization in the God-Man who, as the head of all, gathers all things into a unity.

Teilhard was interested most of all in advancing the understanding of Christ's cosmic lordship (still conceived by Ephe-

---

[27] A. Guggenberger, "Personierende Welt und Inkarnation," in *Hochland* 53 (1960/1), pp. 318-32; "Christus und die Welt nach Teilhard de Chardin," in *Theologie der Gegenwart* 8 (1965), pp. 9-19.
[28] *Idem*, "Christus und die Welt," *loc. cit.*, p. 11.

sians and Colossians in terms of the world-image of antiquity) toward a fresh understanding in harmony with the modern concept of dynamic evolution. This seemed possible to him only if we no longer saw Christ's lordship merely as something beyond the world, something static and complete, but also as something which unfolds itself in the present, inspiring this evolution. "God partially immerses himself in things, by becoming 'element', and then, from this vantage point in the heart of matter, by assuming the control and leadership of what we now call evolution. Christ, principle of universal vitality because sprung up as man among men, put himself in the position (maintained ever since) to subdue under himself, to purify, to direct and superanimate the general ascent of consciousness into which he inserted himself. By a perennial act of communion and sublimation, he aggregates to himself the total psychism of the earth." [29] Texts like this one come under heavy fire from Teilhard's critics. Hans Eduard Hengstenberg, of Bonn, thinks that Teilhard has mired himself in unsolvable contradictions.[30] God cannot immerse himself partially in things because Christ's humanity is not a part of God. Nor can Christ as man direct the progress of evolution because as man Christ is as much subject to the cosmos and to evolution as all of us. If Christ's divine nature is called upon to help this cosmic process, the result will be pantheism. There is at least a suspicion that by securing God's immanence in the world through Christ's humanity Teilhard does not clearly distinguish between the two natures.

Teilhard's identification of the Omega point with the cosmic Christ seems to Hengstenberg equally contradictory. Omega cannot be the last member of an evolutionary chain and stand outside this chain all at the same time. This would be just as impossible as to maintain that something has "become" and has not "become" at the same time. If Omega is simply taken as Christ's humanity, then it cannot, as such, direct the evolution-

[29] P. Teilhard de Chardin, *The Phenomenon of Man* (Harper, 1959), p. 294.

[30] H. E. Hengstenberg, *Evolution und Schöpfung* (Munich, 1963), pp. 147-54.

ary process. If Christ is simultaneously the last phase of cosmic growth and the recapitulating head of the cosmos in the sense of St. Paul, then we are faced with the contradiction that this recapitulating head grows out of what it unites and recapitulates.

Hengstenberg thinks that, fundamentally, Teilhard puts the natural order and the supernatural, creation and salvation, on the same level where they flow into each other. The incarnation becomes for him formally one process with that of the natural universe, or, the other way round, evolution becomes salvation and part of the Christian faith. The result of such a confusion would not be the cosmic Christ whom the Church has long known, but a Christ involved in the origin of the cosmos, a concept that is based on a completely temporal view of the rise of the cosmos, and a consequent adjustment of divine creation and salvation to this purely temporal view.

It seems to me that Hengstenberg's verdict does not do justice to Teilhard's christology. It would not be difficult to criticize the christology of the letter to the Colossians on the same basis of confusion between the two natures and between the natural and supernatural orders. If we seriously consider Teilhard's attempt to translate the cosmic christology of the Bible into the terms of the modern concept of evolution, we will approach him with more care and not use the formulae of Chalcedon and Scholasticism as inflexible yardsticks immune to the vicissitudes of history. Such a total rejection of Teilhard as Hengstenberg indulges in is not very helpful; but this does not mean that his objections, taken by themselves, do not deserve serious discussion.

In fact, Teilhard's concept is problematic from more than one point of view, so that even an open-minded theologian like Hans Urs von Balthasar cannot accept it.[31] Balthasar's main objection is that there seems to be no proper place for the cross in Teilhard's christology. If the movement of the whole world is seen as a continuous ascent, what meaning can God's descent in Christ still have? What is the point of that self-surrender in

[31] Hans Urs von Balthasar, "Die Spiritualität Teilhards de Chardin," in *Wort und Wahrheit* 18 (1963), pp. 339-50.

obedience until death on the cross in shame and abandoned by God? He finds it intolerable that Teilhard "attempts to dispose of this mystery of the self-emptying love of God in this whole system of biological energy". He is shocked by his biological treatment of the incarnation and also by the way Teilhard handles the mystery of love as a matter of "energy" and speaks of the "love-conditioning" (*Amorisation*) of the cosmos, and of the heart of a universalized Christ as the heart of love-conditioned matter. Such expressions are unacceptable to Balthasar. Yet, decisive in his rejection of Teilhard's evolutionary christology is the absence of the cross. The cross symbolizes the fact that there is no place where a synthesis of the world and a judging God can be made. That is why the way of the world and the way of God cannot meet at any point. If Teilhard tries to establish such a meeting point, he is still caught in an unsolvable dilemma: he must either reduce evil in the end to a minimum, in which case the cross loses its power and its meaning; or only a part of the noosphere can risk the approach to God, in which case there is no universal convergence.

These objections cannot be summarily dismissed. They touch the heart of Teilhard's christology, and it is difficult to counter them with quotations from his writings in a convincing way. The question is whether the absence of a theological treatment of the cross in Teilhard constitutes an irreparable and basic lacuna in his synthesis or whether it can still be inserted as an afterthought, somewhat like the message about the cross in the hymn of Colossians which, according to many biblical scholars, was added later.

I cannot decide the question here. But perhaps Karl Rahner provides a way of showing how the relation of Christ's death to his cosmic lordship can be clarified. Rahner wonders whether the separation of body and soul by death indicates an utter severance of man's relation to the universe, so that, after death, the soul passes completely beyond this world, and becomes, so to speak, "a-cosmic".[32] It is conceivable that once the relation-

[32] K. Rahner, *Zur Theologie des Todes. Quaestiones disputatae* 2 (Freiburg i. Br., 1958), p. 20.

ship of the individual body is dissolved, a widening, deepening and continuance of this relationship with the world may take place. In this case the soul would not become a-cosmic at death but would rather develop a relationship with the whole universe. The soul would become more closely and more inwardly related to that real ground of the world which is the foundation of the unity of all things. The thought of such a relation to the cosmos, occasioned by death, is indeed unusual since we commonly imagine that death decisively severs the relation of the soul to the cosmos. But Rahner thinks that, on ontological and theological grounds, the hypothesis is tenable that at death the bodily relation of the soul is extended to the whole universe and that the whole universe takes the place of the individual body.

When we consider in addition that at death man's total activity is incorporated in the cosmos in a lasting and definite way, as a lasting contribution of the individual man to the universe, then we can see that Jesus, too, is freed by death from the limitations of his earthly existence and is established in a lasting relationship to the universe. The spiritual reality of Christ stands open to the whole world through his death and is incorporated in the cosmos as a lasting modification of a real and ontological character.

In this way we can see that the extension of Christ's power to the whole universe is not something mythical derived from gnosticism but is ontologically founded on the fact that Christ's humanity is active in the very depths of the cosmos as a reality which is superior to all other powers.

According to Rahner, such a view might clarify Christ's descent into hell, which we confess in the Apostles' Creed. This should not be imagined so much as a descent in the Sheol of the Old Testament but rather as an entering "into the inner depths of the reality of the world where all things are united at the root".[33] The reality of Christ, fulfilled at his death, would thus become the dominant guiding principle of all created reality. At the same time, Christ would thus become the existential precondition of all created personal life in the universe, since his

[33] *Ibid.*, p. 59.

decisive influence would affect the personal dimension as well as all other cosmic dimensions.

This view is attractive but not easy to prove from Scripture or tradition. If we add to this Rahner's interpretation of christology within the perspective of evolution[34] which had definitely scientific readers in view, it becomes clear how close his view is to the christological intuitions of Teilhard. Rahner himself realizes this but maintains that he reached his view independently of Teilhard.[35]

[34] K. Rahner, "Die Christologie innerhalb einer evolutiven Weltanschauung," in *Schriften zur Theologie* 5 (Einsiedeln, 1962), pp. 183-221.

[35] *Ibid.*, p. 186. After I had finished this article there appeared the essay of Horst Bürkle, "Die Frage nach dem 'kosmischen Christus' als Beispiel einer ökumenisch orientierten Theologie," in *Kerygma und Dogma* 11 (1965), pp. 103-15 in which he shows principally how important the subject of the "cosmic Christ", so long neglected in the theology of the West, has become for the dialogue between Christianity and the religions of East Asia where a new missionary awareness has sprung up. The article was prompted by an address, given by Joseph A. Sittler at New Delhi in 1961 in the plenary assembly of the World Council of Churches where it provoked a lively debate and has since had astonishing repercussions. Sittler based himself on Colossians 1, 15-20, and demanded that the Church abandon the individualistic atmosphere and reintroduce the experience of the world as a whole into her Christian witness. Some theologians, like W. Andersen and G. Rosenkranz, objected and asked whether this would not lead to a misinterpretation of the Christian view of sin, redemption, justification and eschatological expectation. Bürkle rightly points out that this kind of criticism still springs from the old point of view which should be given up precisely in order to bring out again the relation of the Christian message to the whole world. I can only agree with him when, in his opposition to any existentialist-personalist contraction of the kerygma, the author declares: "The event of Christ must be deployed to meet the whole prospect of a world which has become recognizable and significant. Where essential parts of a world-experience fall outside the scope of the faith, the witness loses its missionary strength. In this sense, mission means the uninterrupted occupation and penetration of Christ's claim to universal lordship in a world that is seen in a new light" (p. 108).

The same contact with Eastern thought has given rise to another book which is very different from the theological studies dealt with so far: Arthur Schult, *Das Johannesevangelium als Offenbarung des kosmischen Christus* (Remagen, 1965). It has no scientific or theological pretensions but attempts to unveil the spirit hidden in the text by a meditative interpretation of the whole gospel of St. John. The sources for this meditation are the anthroposophy of Rudolf Steiner, the ideas of a Christian community of Friedrich Rittelmeyer and much material taken from alchemy

As soon as an attempt is made to relate christology to modern science, the question of the universe inevitably turns to Teilhard. Man, with all his secular and religious history, must appear as a negligible by-product of nature within the great cosmic evolution. But we should remember that the universe becomes truly itself only in the spirit, and thus the history of man is not an insignificant, narrow channel within the cosmic stream, but rather the history of the spirit through which the history of the cosmos attains its true meaning.

This must be applied, more explicitly than ever before, to the universe beyond our solar system. All through, the cosmos can realize itself only in spiritual beings related to the world, whatever their condition in space and time. The highest personal synthesis, however, can be achieved only by one spirit, not a multiplicity of spirits. This spirit must embody even the lowest level of its finite condition and be identical with an individual being, with all its limitations. But this spirit must also attain the highest level of universality, since this universalism is the mark of the spirit. But this applies only to Jesus Christ, who recapitulates the whole cosmos in the fullness of time.

---

and astrology. The author also shows the influence of the sophiology of Soloviev and Berdyaev (whose importance for a cosmic christology has also been pointed out by Karl Pfleger in his instructive booklet, *Die verwegenen Christozentriker* [Freiburg i. Br., 1964]), and the teaching of Sri Aurobindos. This syncretizing mixture leads to an understanding of the gospel of St. John as a kind of prelude to the age of the Holy Spirit, which will introduce a reconciliation between the main religions of Asia and Christianity. A dialogue with this type of spirituality is not necessarily sterile, but this would require an explanation of basic principles of Christian thought which altogether exceeds the scope of the subject under discussion.

Olivier Rousseau, O.S.B./*Chevetogne, Belgium*

The Idea of the Kingship of Christ

s a result of St. Paul's christological visions of the cosmos and
the critical updating, by recent
commentators, of Teilhard de Chardin cited at the end of the
preceding article on Christ's reign over all creation,[1] there have
been many changes and developments in Christian thought. Yet,
all this has not succeeded in radically altering the original idea
of the kingdom. This probably shall never occur.

Early liturgies offer profuse orchestrations of the Pauline
texts. The anaphora of St. Mark's Alexandrian liturgy may serve
as an example. Here, to the Isaian temple vision, the trisagion,
is added the idea of Christ's ascension, by which he was raised,
according to Ephesians 1, 21, above every name in this world
and in the world to come. "Truly," we read in this anaphora following the threefold sanctus of the angels, "heaven and earth
are filled with thy holy splendor, through the appearing of our

[1] A. Guggenberger, Egstenberg, H. Urs von Balthasar, K. Rahner, and
the author of the article. To this should be added some French works:
H. de Lubac, *La Pensée religieuse de P. Teilhard de Chardin* (Paris,
1962), esp. p. 194; E. Rideau, *La pensée du Père Teilhard de Chardin*
(Paris, 1965), p. 150 n. 8 (reference to "la parole attendue"—the expectation of the Word); P. Fessard, "La vision religieux et cosmique de
Chardin," in *Mélanges de Lubac* III, p. 239; P. Smulders, *La vision de
Teilhard de Chardin* (Paris, 1964), p. 45; G. Crespy (Protestant), *La
pensée theologique de Teilhard de Chardin* (Paris, 1961).

Lord and Savior Jesus Christ." [2] Commenting on this passage and recalling that the essence of the Church consists precisely in its union with heaven's praise, E. Peterson once wrote: "The worship of the Church is not the liturgy of a human religious society connected with a particular temple, but worship which pervades the whole universe and in which sun, moon and all the stars take part." [3] This is exactly what the anaphora goes on to say.

The praise of the universe is united with the praise of heaven and the angels, "and this is unthinkable apart from the breaking open of heaven by the ascension of Christ" [4] and his enthronement at the Father's right hand. The same author adds: "Man's liturgical act is placed in relation to the whole cosmos. This is not surprising because the redemption itself is an event involving the whole cosmos." This idea, so magnificently expressed in the liturgy of St. Mark, reappears, sometimes merely hinted, sometimes fully developed, in most of the early liturgies. There, its effect is profound, for it is indeed the most perfect expression of Christ's cosmic kingship.

The regions of hell also witnessed his royal victory and his glory. The Oriental liturgies give many examples to illustrate the third term of the Pauline text, "the regions of the earth, and above the earth and beneath the earth". To cite only one, the Byzantine Sunday tropes refer constantly to the paschal mystery and they develop the following themes: "The dead rise, struck by the brightness of eternal life; at Christ's coming, the gates of hell yield to the terror and open of their own accord; the angels are transfixed in wonder, the demons are filled with terror; hell vomits and rejects its prisoners; it is stripped like a vanquished enemy." [5]

Christ will also reign on earth. If, as has been written, the

[2] Cf. E. Peterson, *The Angels and the Liturgy* (New York, 1964), p. 21; "La Liturgie du ciel et de la terre," in *Irénikon* 14 (1937), pp. 147ff.

[3] *The Angels and the Liturgy, op. cit.,* p. 22.

[4] *Ibid.,* p. 23.

[5] See the texts cited in our study: "La Descente aux Enfers dans le cadre des liturgies chrétiennes," in *La Maison-Dieu* 43 (1955), pp. 104ff., especially pp. 109-10.

eschatological view of the apocalypse gave "a certain political coloring to the final victory of the Lord Jesus" [6] (his faithful ones have refused to serve the kings of the earth in order to be subject to him), the Christians of the first three centuries saw in Christ's reign—*Kyrios Christos*—the realization in a transposed realm of the messianic prophecies of the kingdom.

Furthermore, writers of Christian antiquity had also placed the person of Christ at the midpoint of history, just as they believed Jerusalem to be the geographical center of the world. Actually, in 525, Dionysius Exiguus in the preface of his book, *Liber de Paschate*, established a date that was to have great influence when he calculated the number of years since the incarnation of the Word so that "the *exordium* of our hope might be accented, and the cause of man's renewal shine with greater brilliance".[7] This was an affirmation of a form of Christ's supratemporal kingship. Today when non-believers date their actions according to the Christian calendar they implicitly confess this kingship: "Every knee shall bow."

Millenarian ideas were based on these facts, and a combination of heavenly and earthly kingdoms led to a modification of the great Pauline concept. Although the Nicaean-Constantinople creed insisted, against Marcel of Ancyra, on the perennial nature of Christ's kingdom ("and of his kingdom there shall be no end"), beginning with the Constantinian era the kingship of Christ on this earth was to be manifested in a new way and, speaking frankly, in a less spiritual way. The emperor of the new Rome became a Christian and transferred to his person the religious prerogatives of paganism and made himself "Christ's representative on earth". "He was the elect of God and as such the lord and master, but he was also the living symbol of the Christian empire entrusted to him by God." [8]

The emperors attributed to themselves such titles as: *En*

---

[6] J. Cambier, "La Seigneurie du Christ sur son Eglise et sur le monde d'apres le N.T.," in *Irénikon* 30 (1957), p. 390.

[7] Cf. my article: "Les Pères et la théologie du temps," in *La Maison-Dieu* 30 (1952), pp. 36ff. Cf. also O. Cullmann, *Christ and Time* (Philadelphia, 1950).

[8] G. Ostrogorsky, *Histoire de l'Etat byzantin* (Paris, 1956), p. 57.

Christō basileus, en Christō autokrator.[9] Although they were consecrated by the Church, the two powers, the spiritual and the temporal, were for a long time united and could not always be distinguished. The origin of Christ's kingship on earth was linked with political power. It has been said, with good reason, that the eschatological dimensions of this Byzantine concept had their theological consequences, because ultimately the Christian city had no meaning except in terms of the kingdom of the Christ who is to come.[10] Yet, this insight eventually lost its force and was limited by the Church herself. Could it be understood of Charlemagne's empire and of its feudal divisions?

The emperor of the West was not given a share in the monopoly claimed by Constantine's successors because the Byzantines believed that there could be only one emperor just as there could be only one God. In the West the consecration of emperors and kings by members of the hierarchy was an invitation to further Christ's reign on earth rather than to represent him.[11] This was especially true because after this time princes were closely united by a most powerful religious bond, the papacy, which asserted its dominion over them; and soon it was the concept of Christ's kingship in his vicar, the pope, that triumphed. It has been proved that beginning in the 12th century the expression, "the pope, the vicar of Christ" was used throughout the Church and replaced the older formula, "the vicar of Peter".[12]

The struggle between the two powers highlighted this idea which was to become and is today one of the most sensitive areas of Western theology. Obviously in these perspectives little heed was paid to Christ's cosmic kingship. Yet, in no part of the Church was it ever completely forgotten. Proof of this is to

---

[9] Boeckius, *Corpus Inscriptionum graecarum* IV, nn. 8673-8.

[10] E. Lanne, "Le laicat dans l'Eglise ancienne," in *Verbum Caro* 71-72 (1964), p. 116.

[11] *Ordo Romanus* XIV, in *Patrologia Latina* 78, col. 1240. Cf. C. Bouman, *Sacring and Crowning* (Groningen, 1857), p. 187: "In hoc regni solio . . . regnare faciat Jesus Christus."

[12] M. Maccarone, *Vicarius Christi* (Rome, 1952), Chap. IV: "Vicarius Christi, titolo papale (XIIe-XIIIe sec.)."

be found in cupola representations of the Byzantine *Pantokrator* and in medieval iconography.[13]

Christ's Kingship in Medieval Theology

Dom J. Leclercq has shown how highly 13th-century theologians valued the idea of Christ's kingship. He says that at that time "exegetes and other doctors stressed the kingship of Christ and his many different titles, as God equal in power to his Father, as incarnate Word, as heir of the Davidic dynasty, as fulfillment of the messianic prophecies, and finally as redeemer who triumphed over the devil, sin and man through his passion and resurrection".[14]

Yet for a long time it was necessary to keep this doctrine in step with the struggle between the two powers. On one side "the imperialists did not fail to claim for the emperor . . . dominion over the 'kingdom of the Church' "; on the other side, "the most ardent spirits knew that Christ's kingship pointed to that of the Church and the pope".[15] In fact, a century later the doctrine of Christ's royal power led to a diminution of the spiritual character of the Church. This was the result of the misfortunes connected with the Great Schism. Then the idea of Christ's kingship was transformed into an ecclesiology pure and simple. Rather than attribute the power of a vicar to persons from whom one was alienated because of their conflicts—emperors, kings, popes—it was the Church as queen and mother who was recognized as possessing these powers. Not only was she described as "the dwelling of the great king" (she was called the *basilica* because she was the dwelling place of the eternal king, the *basileus*), not only was she recognized as the city of the great king, not only was she acknowledged as his spouse, but she was also

[13] Cf. C. Capizzi, "Pantokrator," in *Orientalia Christiana Analecta* 170 (1964); F. Van der Meer, *Majestas Domini* (Città del Vaticano, 1938).

[14] J. Leclercq, *L'idée de la Royauté du Christ au Moyen Age* (Paris, 1959), pp. 29ff.; cf. also F. Kempf, "Die katholische Lehre von der Gewalt der Kirche über das Zeitliche in ihrer geschichtlichen Entwicklung seit dem Investiturstreit," in *Catholica* 12 (1958), pp. 50ff.

[15] Leclercq, *op. cit.*, p. 41.

acclaimed as royalty. "Queen of the Christian people, she stands always at the right hand of her Spouse. She shares in his power. Christ assists her as he assisted the Blessed Virgin, the mother of the supreme king and the queen of the triumphant Church." [16]

There were other consequences to these doctrinal adjustments. The Church, overly "spiritualized", became at the same time more democratic in her conciliar theory, because the council was the visible expression of the invisible Church. "The Church is queen," Gerson wrote, "but the pope is not the king; he is a subject of the Church." By a strange deviation of an exaggerated theory of collegiality, another author, Bernard of Rouzergue, wrote: "It was to the cardinals that Christ, the King of kings, the Lord of lords, entrusted his power. It is they and not the pope who possess the right to convoke the council." [17] Clearly a rereading of these texts shows that certain past anxieties have reappeared today.

It is apparent that Christ's kingship could have had no cosmic dimension in the theology of that period. Nor is it surprising that these new insights influenced the Reformers and led to at least a partial rejection of the sacramental hierarchical visibility of the Church.

Contemporary Theology and the Kingship of Christ

Yet this is not to say that theologians, in recent centuries, attempted to develop a complete theory of Christ's kingship. It is understandable that scientific research and discoveries raised new questions requiring new answers. What could come of all this? Let us begin with a brief summary of what contemporary theology has said about Christ's kingship.

One of the major Catholic documents on this subject is the encyclical *Quas primas* of Pius XI (December 11, 1925) issued on the occasion of the institution of the feast of Christ the King.[18] Yet it contains no allusion to Christ's cosmic king-

[16] *Ibid.*, pp. 195-6.
[17] *Ibid.*, p. 197.
[18] The French text may be found in *Documentation Catholique* (1926), p. 259. The English text may be found (among other places) in *The*

ship because the purpose of the feast was to stress Christ's rule over men, over human intellects and wills and hearts.[19]

About the same time one big ecumenical conference after another stressed Christ's kingship. In the first Life and Work Conference at Stockholm, August 19-30, 1925, two opposing tendencies could be discerned. Let us label them the transcendent and the immanent aspects. There was, on the one hand, the heavenly and the eschatological vision, and on the other, the vision of things of this world. Both visions were developed with a new dynamism and pointed toward a progressive liberation, ignoring the completely outmoded question of temporal power.

In November, 1925, Pastor C. Scheer gave a detailed description of the Stockholm Conference in "Le christianisme sociale". This is what he has to say about those who hold the first theory: "The Kingdom of God is completely supernatural. It is God's sovereign work. It moves in a sphere utterly unlike anything that men may achieve by their own efforts. The world, the work of civilization, politics, economics—all these have what the Germans call their *Eigengesetzlichkeit,* that is, their special laws, the immanent exigencies, springing from their proper nature and to which it is impossible to give a completely Christian character. . . ." For those who, on the contrary, seek immanence:

Encyclicals of Pius XI, ed. J. H. Ryan, pp. 129-56. A few years later the same Pontiff, Pius XI, through the Lateran agreement (1929), put an end to the theory of the temporal power of the Church. This was the first step toward what is called today the end of the Age of Constantine.

[19] The purpose of this feast was to combat the laicism that began in the 19th century and continued into the 20th, by restoring to Christ the place the modern world had taken from him and to "rediscover a civilization which would be convinced that all things are subject to the Son of God". A. Vonier, *The Victory of Christ* (London, 1934). Cf. C. Duquoc, "La royauté de Christ," in *Lumière et Vie* 57 (1962), p. 84. Cf. also the other articles in this issue devoted to Christ the King: J. Giblet, "Jesus, Fils de David"; A. George, "La Seigneurie du Christ sur le monde (translation of *Geist und Leben* [1957], pp. 246ff.); cf. also the April, 1964 issue of *La Vie Spirituelle* on "La royauté pascale du Christ"; M. Thurian, "Jesus est Seigneur"; J. Bouyer, "Royauté cosmique"; J. Comblin, "Tu l'as dit, Je suis Roi", etc.; J. Leclercq, "La Royauté du Christ dans la spiritualité française du XVe siècle," in *Suppl. la Vie spir.* (1947), pp. 216-22, 291-307.

"The Kingdom of God, although it cannot be realized without help from above, is nevertheless the goal of human efforts. Little by little this kingdom, through our work and our prayers, is meant to transform civilization by progressively eliminating all that unregenerate nature has introduced." And the author concludes with these words: "In making these observations the Stockholm Conference has rendered a service to Christianity. It has squarely confronted us with the true problem. Yes, this does not mean that we have to find out whether in the future we will be more active, more socialistic, democratic or pacifist. But here is the question to which the Churches will have to answer by their attitude: Do we know how to maintain, affirm and establish the fundamental paradox of the Gospel, that consists in powerfully influencing, dominating, transforming and permeating civilization without ever identifying itself with this civilization or losing itself in it?" [20]

As we have said, the idea of the kingship of God and of Christ was basic to all the practical resolutions adopted at Stockholm,[21] and was at the root of all the differences expressed there. The two tendencies became more and more pronounced and were present in all the big ecumenical conferences. Forty years later

[20] *La Conference du Christianisme pratique à Stockholm* (*Le Christianisme social*, Oct.-Nov., 1925, pp. 929-33 *passim*); cf. also G. Thils, *Histoire doctrinale du mouvement oecumenique* (Louvain, 1963), pp. 27-8. The dominant concern expressed at the close of the last work cited above is "the evangelical penetration of civilization". The idea became increasingly important in the theology of earthly realities and has found in the theories of Teilhard de Chardin the possibility of a new vision of Christ's kingship. This provides an antidote to the development of the Marxist mystique and *Weltanschauung*.)

[21] In 1924 Archbishop Solderblom, at the time of the preparation of the Stockholm Conference which he was organizing, made the following remark: "We see a confrontation between two basic concepts of the kingdom or rather the reign of God. Is God's reign a force immanent in mankind, an energetic and enthusiastic program for our activity? Or, is God's reign the judgment and salvation brought about by God in an inscrutable way during the course of history and in its fulfillment, a divine activity before which we should bow and adore, even when our poor intelligence understands nothing?" "Impressions dominantes," in *Le Christianisme social* (1925), p. 852; cf. *Irénikon* 14 (1937), p. 187.

this is still true. The leaders have not yet resolved this problem which is a clear proof that Christ and his victory continue to be "the great question of the world", *magna quaestio mundi,* according to a medieval expression.

Helmut Riedlinger, in another article in this volume, mentions that the representatives of the young Afro-Asian Churches reproached European Protestantism for centuries of neglect of Christ's cosmic dimension. Let us investigate how they wanted this question to be expressed today.

Naturally the Stockholm Conference accented "earthly realities" because of the Life and Work program. But as early as 1927 the Faith and Order Conference at Lausanne approached the question of "the Church and the world" very differently and explored entirely different problems. It should quickly be noted that the development of these questions was due largely to the powerful influence of the Orthodox theologians. First at Stockholm, then at Lausanne, but most especially at the two 1937 conferences at Oxford (Life and Work) and Edinburgh (Faith and Order), attention was drawn to their anthropology and to its cosmic ramifications in christology.

In his remarkable study, *The Kingship of Jesus Christ,* Dr. Visser 't Hooft, the General Secretary of the Ecumenical Center (Geneva), pointed out that the Russian theologians had made a rich contribution to great ecumenical conferences. "Thanks to them," he wrote, "European theology was placed in contact with the great current of Christian thought in which had been preserved the eschatological vision of the primitive Church untouched by the reduction of secularization proper to the history of Western Europe. Their vast theological systems were received with reserve and much criticism but they greatly contributed to the widening of the horizons of European theology and the return to the universal Gospel of the primitive Church. The Orthodox Church, in the paschal liturgy, prays in these words: 'All creation celebrates Christ's resurrection on which (the Church) is founded.' It was this Orthodox insight into the cosmic meaning of Christ's victory that enriched Western theology." [22]

It is immediately evident that such a significant orientation, let us rather say a discovery, could have far-reaching consequences on the development of the ecumenical movement.[23] However, the progress of these renewed understandings was slow. The questions, at least, had been raised, and, as a result, they were later to be examined in depth.

Roman Catholic Thought on the Kingship of Christ

There was also the same renewal in the Catholic Church thanks to "the return to the sources" and the study of the history of theology. This was especially true during the postwar years (1945 and after) when the writings of many different Christian and non-Christian religions were widely circulated. One of the most influential collections for those speaking French was the interdenominational review *Dieu Vivant*.[24]

During the ten years that this review appeared, it was the Russian thinkers and theologians (almost all of these men lived in Paris: Lossky, Berdyaev, Boulgakoff, Lot-Borodine, Arseniev, Zander, Florovsky, Zenkovsky, Schmemann) who were considered to have a wide influence and to be among its most original collaborators. Many of these authors and others who took part in this movement (Peterson, Casel, Daniélou, Bouyer) attempted to explain the divine transcendence and to show the importance of Christ's total kingship by freeing this concept of all abstractions and treating it existentially.

Although they sometimes went to extremes they were nevertheless not without influence on the ecumenical movement. There the dialectic of earthly and eschatological realities is still maintained by a kind of confrontation which did not succeed in securing the triumph of one element over the other.

[22] W. Visser 't Hooft, *La Royauté de Jésus-Christ* (Geneva, 1948), pp. 43-4; conferences conducted as the Stone Lectures at Princeton in 1947.
[23] Cf. especially G. Aulen, *Christus Victor. La notion chrétienne de rédemption* (Paris: Ed. franc., 1949); R. Leivestad, *Christ the Conqueror* (London, 1954).
[24] Cf. *Dieu Vivant* 1 (1945), p. 9.

To understand the development of the obsessive concerns of these theologians it would be necessary to examine—but we cannot do this—the Acts of the great ecumenical assemblies and the conferences of their committees since the 1948 meeting in Amsterdam.[25]

The theme of the Evanston Conference in 1954, "Christ, the Only Hope of the World", certainly did not minimize eschatology.[26] The next conference chose the theme: "Christ, the Light of the World". It met in New Delhi and addressed itself to these problems. At the preparatory consultative meeting at Arnoldsheim in July, 1956, a detailed study was begun on "Christ's Lordship over the World and the Church". The subtitles are evocative: (1) The meaning of the world; (2) The relation between the creative lordship of God who judges and sustains the universe and the redemptive lordship of God manifested in Jesus Christ; (3) Christ's victory over the "powers"— How are we to understand them in the modern world? (4) How God makes use of the rebellion of his adversaries and of disobedience to accomplish his plan; (5) Christ's lordship over the world and the Church's mission in the world.[27]

Beginning in 1954, a group of Catholic theologians, under the direction of Msgr. Willebrands, presently Bishop and Secretary of the Roman Secretariat for Unity, began a series of studies parallel to those of the great ecumenical Assemblies. In *Istina* may be read a paper on Christian hope sent to Evanston.[28] A

---

[25] The theme of the Amsterdam Assembly, "The disorder of man and the plan of God", which was developed most particularly by Karl Barth, had, as all know, a marked influence over the whole theology of transcendence in Protestantism and elsewhere. Cf. L. Lialine, "Le dialogue théologique à Amersterdam," in *Irénikon* 23 (1950), pp. 133ff. On the Barthian influence, cf. J. Ellet, *Fausse présence au monde moderne* (Coll. Les bergers et les mages, 1963), chap. I: "La conformisation de l'Eglise au monde moderne."

[26] Cf. L. Lialine, "Evanston-Etudes," in *Irénikon* 28 (1955), pp. 363ff.

[27] Cf. "Conference consultative d'Arnoldshain," in *Istina* 3 (1956), pp. 473ff. and *ibid.*, 5 (1958), p. 226: "L'Eglise et le souverain domaine du Christ sur toutes choses." The enormous mass of all kinds of documents, printed and mimeographed, may be obtained from the *Division des Etudes* of COE (Conseil Oecuménique des Eglises) at Geneva.

[28] "Le Christ, l'Eglise et la grâce dans l'économie de l'espérance chré-

little later (1958) an important article on the lordship of Christ over the Church and the world was prepared for the New Delhi Conference.[29] It was signed by a group of theologians of the Catholic Conference for Ecumenical Questions.

The last general assembly of the World Council, taking place in Montreal in 1963, took as the first point of its program "The Church in God's Plan", and opened with the subject: "Christ, the New Creation". It may be summarized in these words: "Jesus Christ is Lord and Savior. But he is the immolated lamb who remains forever the one who is raised up, the one who is crucified. The Church should be considered as the crucified and risen Body of Christ whose existence is determined by the participation in the death and resurrection of him who is her head. In this way the Church is a new creation and shows this by the obedience of a disciple and the fidelity of a servant in the world. The testimony of Christ's victory over the 'rebellious powers' brings suffering and humiliation to the Church. It is the freedom of the children of God, the freedom of the disciples of Christ crucified and risen, that makes possible a new solidarity with all God's creatures. Christ calls us and frees us so that we can be truly and totally men in a secularized world. Christians are also free to rejoice wholeheartedly at each encounter with signs of God's grace and truth in the created order. In this connection it

---

tienne," in *Istina* 1 (1954), pp. 132ff.; C. Dumont, "Réflexions sur l'Assemblée oecuménique d'Evanston," *ibid.*, p. 311.

[29] This was published in *Istina* 6 (1959), pp. 131ff. At the Chevetogne Conferences in 1957 the theme of Christ's lordship over the world was developed. The same theme was repeated at a small conference at Istina, then discussed once more at the *Conference catholique pour les Questions oecuméniques* at Paderborn in 1959. The report appeared in *Istina* in 1959. The chief author was Father Congar. An important bibliography was added, including Catholic studies of Christ's lordship (see the same number of *Istina*). The following works should be added to this bibliography: H. Urs von Balthasar, *Herrlichkeit, eine theologische Aesthetik* I (Einsiedeln, 1961), chap. V. French edition: *La gloire et la Croix* 1, chap. V, "Le Christ, centre de la figure de revelation"; J. Groot, "De vestiging van het Rijk Gods," in *Jaarboek voor het werkgenootschap van katholieke theologen in Nederland*, 1958; P. Lengsfeld, *Adam und Christus. Die Adam-Christustypologie im neuen Testament und ihre dogmatische Verwendung bei M. Scheeben und K. Barth* (Essen, 1965).

is plain that the question of the relation of creation and redemption should be studied promptly and in depth within the limits of faith and the constitution. Lastly certain relevant questions are addressed to the Churches along the following lines: 'The Church is the body of the crucified Lord; can it expect to be treated in any other way than he?' " [30]

The emphasis placed on *kenosis* (self-emptying) in Christ's work is perhaps surprising and is not altogether in harmony with the teaching of the great Christian liturgies. More importance should be attached to the idea of the resurrection. But let us recall that research about these movements is still in process.

Conclusion

There are some who would like to see a new theology of Christ's kingship over the visible and tangible cosmos. Toward what goal is the evolution of the world directed? Is man preparing for the kingdom? And if he is, does this mean that there will or will not be an eschatological sundering?[31] Teilhard de Chardin's attempt to synthesize the two tendencies, by giving a christological and Pauline direction to the development of the world, to man's work and even to the matter of the work itself, has brought new enthusiasm and courage to a whole generation which had long been groping for answers to these problems.

Still, the Gospel message has been engrafted on the old Judaeo-Christian culture which had been prepared for this event. This culture has grown in complete harmony with the great inspiration of the prophets; the Word of God resonates here. Have eschatological visions closed in on the Word and locked it in their myth? As a matter of fact, it is through firm belief in the Word that we are certain to attain to the truth about our mysterious end, and it is with the help of the Word that we will persevere in faith.

Moreover, we should refuse to make any effort to correlate

[30] S. Strotmann, "Le Mouvement *Foi et Constitution* à Montreal, 12-26 juillet 1963," in *Irénikon* 36 (1963), pp. 377-8.

[31] Y. Congar, *Lay People in the Church* (Westminster, Md.: The Newman Press, 1957).

our progress with the advance of science which is always in a
state of flux. Christian culture is sacred and inspired. It is part
of the vesture of the unchanging Word. We should draw near
this Word with childlike simplicity because in going deeper into
the Word we breathe an air that transcends us and which we
need to strengthen our hope. Telescopes and cosmic-cameras do
not replace the naked eye or the joys of vision; nor will science
ever replace faith.

Interplanetary space, the planets themselves, and their movements may seem very different from what we call, in biblical
terms, "the sun, the moon and the stars" which, with the angels
and the heavenly court, are like the other side of an invisible
world where God reigns and where Christ returned after his
victory. But this imagery has also been given us by God.

We need not read very far in the gospels to discover that all
human effort is inevitably woven into that ontologically good
network of finality which advances (or delays) the consummation of the Kingdom.

How much more than this can we say? Father Teilhard asked
himself this question. Of course his vision went beyond this
earth. But if, as he says, "the power of the Incarnate Word
penetrates matter itself; it descends into the deepest depths of
the inferior forces"; and if on the other hand, "the Incarnation
will be complete only when the part of a chosen substance contained in every object . . . has rejoined the final Centre of its
completion. *Quid est quod ascendit, nisi quod prius descendit,
ut repleret omnia?*" [32]—then in his investigation properly so
called, only this earth and man at its center seem to have been
the field of his activity.[33]

One truth is manifest from all that has been said. The pseudo-
millenarianism which was identified with the Constantinian era
and its extensions is no longer recognized. Henceforth, Christ's

[32] *The Divine Milieu* (New York, 1960), p. 30.
[33] The last work of Teilhard de Chardin in which these ideas are
touched upon is *Ecrits du temps de guerre* (Paris, 1965), especially the
first chapter, "La vie cosmique," dedicated to *Terra mater* and, through
it, above all to Jesus Christ.

kingship is not to be identified with any temporal power and it has now been purified from any taint of this kind in spite of powerful and still militant forces. Furthermore, all Christians, whatever be the denomination to which they belong, are together striving to recapture the original meaning of this kingship in all its fullness. This is the trend to be found in the declarations of the great ecumenical conferences which we have examined, as well as in the new conciliar texts of Vatican Council II. The Constitution on the Church, at least in its first two chapters, is equally explicit. For example, we read there that: "Since the kingdom of Christ is not of this world (cf. John 18, 36), the Church or People of God in establishing that kingdom takes nothing away from the temporal welfare of any people. Rather does it foster and adopt, insofar as they are good, the ability, riches and customs of each people. Taking them to itself it purifies, strengthens, elevates and consecrates them" (§13b).[34]

Thus in many places a coherent, dynamic and optimistic doctrine is being shaped whose riches are perhaps still hidden from us but in which we dare to believe we will not be disappointed.

[34] This is also true of Schema 13, not yet published, whose contents are already known as this is being written. I am alluding to paragraphs 44 and 45 where the question of the cosmos is linked with the fate of man and Christ's universal lordship.

PART III

DOCUMENTATION
CONCILIUM

Office of the Executive Secretary
Nijmegen, Netherlands

Herbert Vorgrimler/*Freiburg, W. Germany*

The Significance of
Christ's Descent into Hell

For the past twenty years the question of Christ's descent into hell has been dealt with in a variety of ways[1] by various theologians such as Aloys Grillmeier,[2] Hans Urs von Balthasar[3] and Karl Rahner.[4] And yet, even today there exists no proper treatment which would incorporate the relevant results of patrology and put the whole question in the context of modern theology. One may well ask whether such a systematic treatment is even desirable. Modern preaching and catechetics are not interested. Although it is one of the articles of the faith, it has happened before that one or another article has been allowed to rest for a while in the awareness of the Church. The reason for this was not always the spiritual apathy of the ordinary Christian. If the descent is treated in such a

---

[1] There is some bibliography in H. Vorgrimler, "Vorfragen zur Theologie des Karsamstags: Paschatis Sollemnia," in *Festschrift J. A. Jungmann*, ed. by B. Fischer and J. Wagner (Freiburg, 1959), pp. 13-22, and in A. Grillmeier, "Höllenabstieg Christi," in *Lexikon für Theologie und Kirche* V, pp. 450-5.

[2] A. Grillmeier, "Der Gottessohn im Totenreich," in *Zeitschrift für katholische Theologie* 71 (1949), pp. 1-53 and 184-203.

[3] See especially H. Urs von Balthasar, "Eschatologie," in *Fragen der Theologie heute*, ed. by J. Feiner, J. Trütsch and F. Böckle (Einsiedeln, [3]1960), pp. 403-22, esp. pp. 409f.

[4] K. Rahner, "Karsamstag," in *Geist und Leben* 30 (1957), pp. 81-4; *idem*, "Auferstehung des Fleisches," in *Schriften zur Theologie* II, pp. 211-25, esp. pp. 220f.

stepmotherly fashion in theology, preaching and meditation, the main culprit is perhaps that schoolish theology (not to be confused with the best of scholasticism) of fifty or sixty years back which flattered itself that it could give rather too precise answers about the beyond.

Whatever the case may be, my intention is not to reinstate a "forgotten truth" but rather to show that Christ's descent into hell is a decisive juncture at which the main lines of any Christian theology converge. It is a point which lies at the center of theology, not on the periphery. This is all I am concerned with, and not with the reasons why a systematic theology of the descent has failed.

I

BRIEF SKETCH OF THE DEVELOPMENT OF THE DOGMA

Even a severely critical approach to the sources for this dogma shows an astonishingly broad tradition. The classical references are 1 Peter 3, 18ff.; 4, 6; these texts are linked in the debate with Matthew 12, 40; 27, 51; Luke 23, 42f.; Acts 2, 24 and 27; Romans 10, 7; Ephesians 4, 8ff.; Hebrews 13, 20 and Apocalypse 1, 18. The latest commentary on Peter by that expert on patristic exegesis, K. H. Schelkle, finds that, apart from the references in 1 Peter, the descent into hell is always mentioned in connection with Romans 10, 7, Ephesians 4, 8ff. and Hebrews 13, 20.[5] The teaching about the descent appeared in the synods of 358 and 360, and was inserted in the creed before 370 at Aquileia,[6] where it was phrased as "descendit ad inferna", while the *Quicumque* (written about 500 in southern Gaul) used the words "descendit ad inferos". This may suffice to establish that it is part of the "rule of faith". Grillmeier collected the patristic material in the work referred to above and has for the first time

[5] K. Schelkle, *Die Petrusbriefe. Der Judasbrief* (Freiburg, ²1964).
[6] A. Grillmeier, "Höllenabstieg . . . ," p. 454.

attempted an explanation, but the evidence from the liturgical sources has so far not received adequate treatment.[7]

It would be interesting to have not just a historical but a theological analysis of patristic thought about the descent into hell so that we could check the mentality and validity of the work done by these early theologians on the texts of the New Testament. This would be the more important because the modern inclination to demythologize has produced some already current but oversimplified ideas that demand revision. Many modern theologians, including some Catholic ones, are a little too ready to look on present-day theology mainly as a process of constant clearing and cleaning. It is possible that unconsciously they have given the impression that the biblical texts about the descent into hell were purely mythological and that we are now in a position to dispense with it.

But if we look a little more closely into the matter we see that, as the Fathers developed it, this theological question reverses its direction. At first, this theology was interested only in the kerygma, the operative proclamation of salvation which Jesus took into the underworld. Grillmeier calls this the "kerygmatic" and "baptismal" motif. Toward the end of the sixth century, this has become the battle of Jesus in the underworld, or, with even richer fantasy, his bargaining with the devil for souls; and so theological interest was focused on a point which the Church had to reject.[8] The "battle" motif, as Grillmeier calls it, linked the theology of the descent into hell closely with the myths of comparative religion, while the Christian "kergymatic" motif had no link with comparative religion.[9]

In certain circumstances we see, therefore, that a process of progressive mythologization going on in Christian theology can be studied in the theology of the descent as a paradigm. In

---

[7] Cf., however, O. Rousseau, "La descente aux enfers dans le cadre des liturgies chrétiennes," in *Maison-Dieu* 43 (1955), pp. 104-23.

[8] Cf. F. Diekamp, *Die origenistischen Streitigkeiten im sechsten Jahrhundert* (Münster, 1899), particularly pp. 88-98.

[9] A. Grillmeier, "Höllenabstieg . . . ," p. 453.

connection with this we cannot ignore the continuous rise of twentieth century myths in which C. G. Jung was so interested toward the end of his life. However this may be, it is regrettable, in view of the sources and the tradition of the early Church, that so little attention has been paid by theology to the descent into hell. A comparison with any analogous topics of the Bible and their actuality for today will show that they are all taken as more important than the descent. One has but to think of the fall of the angels, mentioned as a warning example in Jude and 2 Peter,[10] to see how normal catechetics today uses it in order to force the history of salvation in principle, and *a priori,* into a system of antagonistic dualism. And the fall of the angels is not even an article of the creed.

II

The Descent into Hell as Related to Certain Vital Theological Issues

I want to point out now which central themes of theology are linked with Christ's descent into hell and how it can throw light on them.

1. Christ's descent into hell implies basic questions which concern the theology of man. First among these is the question of the nature of body and soul and their mutual relationship, particularly in the case of Jesus. The older theology maintains that the corpse of Christ remained in the tomb until the third day while his soul was "located" in the underworld (thus, for instance, Bellarmine). Are these statements of Christian anthropology to be taken literally? Here we must not forget that they still reflect the great christological controversies of the first centuries: Apollinaris and his followers denied that Christ had a human soul and maintained that the Word itself descended into hell, while orthodox theology, in order to protect the full humanity of Christ, taught that Christ's soul descended into hell.

But we should not overlook the reason why this interpreta-

[10] K. Schelkle, *op. cit.,* at the appropriate texts.

tion was taught: it was to secure the full humanity of Christ. If this complete humanity of Christ is in danger, then it is legitimate to secure it with the help of all the categories of anthropology. But between the time of the old Apollinarian controversies and a certain more modern scholasticism the question shifted ground. A rather recent German theologian[11] blandly formulated the problem as follows: the Christian teaching about the descent into hell came about "through the need to answer the question where Christ's soul could be in the time between death and resurrection". This is too glib to be true. Straightforward historical research shows that this teaching was certainly not inspired by modern curiosity where Christ's soul might have been during those three days. Is it too blunt to say that the question of the "location" of the various "parts" of Christ during those three days is typical of the bogus problems conjured up by modern rationalism?

Moreover, the question of the "three days" is still far from solved.[12] To which writings does Paul refer in 1 Corinthians 15, 4 according to which Christ rose on the third day? What do we make of the fact that Jesus foretold his resurrection according to Mark "after three days", according to Luke "on the third day" and according to Matthew variously "on the third day" and "after three days"? Is it meant to be a scriptural proof taken from Hosea 6, 2, or does the number of three days simply indicate an extraordinarily short space of time, the interval during which God comes to the assistance of the just, according to contemporary Judaism? Do these "three days" really prompt a need to explain where the various parts of Jesus were during that interval and what he did during that time? Moreover, this division of Christ, mentioned in the older theology, cannot be taken too literally. When, for instance, the fourth Council of the

[11] J. Pohle, *Lehrbuch der Dogmatik,* 1902; newly reedited by J. Gummersbach (Paderborn, [10]1956). The quotation will be found in Vol. 2, p. 280.

[12] K. Lehmann has written an excellent exegetical thesis for his licentiate with E. Dhanis in 1964: *Auferweckt am dritten Tage gemäss den Schriften,"* which I hope to incorporate in the series *Quaestiones disputatae.*

Lateran declares: "He descended in his soul and rose again in the flesh and ascended in both together" (*descendit in anima et resurrexit in carne ascenditque pariter in utroque,* Denzinger, 429), this can hardly mean that the Lord rose only in the flesh and without his soul. So we see that in the descent of Christ into hell the theological teachings about the "body", the "soul" and about what happens to both, converge.[13]

So we must be allowed to ask the question: are we wholly forbidden to say that Jesus Christ (without further division) descended into the realm of the dead? No doubt, in 1 Peter 3, 19, we are told that Christ descended into the underworld "in the *Pneuma*". But can this pneumatic man of the New Testament (who also creates serious problems elsewhere, as in 1 Corinthians 5, 5) be totally identified with our Aristotelian soul? If we leave Paul out of it for the moment, this does not seem the case in 1 Peter. For, in 1 Peter 3, 18, we read that he was "put to death in the flesh, but made alive in the spirit". And of those to whom Christ brought the kerygma in the underworld, 1 Peter 4, 6 says: "For this is why the gospel was preached even to the dead, that though judged in the flesh like men, they might live in the spirit like God." Why does the text not say that Jesus was also made alive in the "flesh"? The question is important because, in contrast to our case as sinful men, the *sarx* or "flesh" cannot refer in Jesus to that part of the person which has fallen prey to sin and needs purifying. It would be an oversimplification to say that *sarx* in the New Testament refers to the whole man as given over to the world and hostile to God, while *pneuma* (spirit) would refer to the whole man as justified and endowed with God's grace. The text of 1 Peter teaches us to bestow a little more care on the problem. Moreover, the other texts which

[13] Elements of a modern theological anthropology can be found in the articles "Leib" and "Seele" by J. Metz, in *Lexikon für Theologie und Kirche* VI, pp. 902-5 and IX, pp. 570-3 (with bibliography); see esp. also P. Overhage and K. Rahner, *Das Problem der Hominisation* (Freiburg, ³1965) and K. Rahner, *Zur Theologie des Todes* (Freiburg, ⁴1963). American editions: *Hominisation: The Evolutionary Origin of Man as a Theological Problem* (Herder and Herder, 1965); *On the Theology of Death* (Herder and Herder, 1961).

speak of the descent (Rom. 10, Eph. 4 and Heb. 13) make no special mention of the *pneuma* of Christ, but simply speak of Jesus.

I cannot believe that the genuine statements of the magisterium about the descent forbid us to say that the whole Jesus descended into hell as long as we do not deny the presence there of his soul. If Matthew 12, 40, refers to the descent at all, it does not contradict this point since it simply mentions the "Son of man", and not the soul of the Son of man. Nor is the point contradicted by the time indication "after three days" or "on the third day" because the point of the Easter narratives is not to fix the exact time when Jesus' body was glorified, but rather to indicate an interval after which Jesus arose on this earth, i.e., appeared to the Apostles in his glorified body.

The glorified body itself is described in various ways, by the Synoptics, Paul, and John, as so spiritual [14] that it is difficult to see why we cannot simply say with Romans, Ephesians, Hebrews and the creed that Jesus was present in the underworld. Such a statement would fit in very well with the ideas of Semitic anthropology: man lives as a whole or man is dead as a whole in the underworld. For an explanation of this from the point of view of modern anthropology I may refer to Karl Rahner's theology of death.[15] According to him, death does not deprive the human soul of all relation to matter, but rather intensifies this relationship in a new form.

This theology takes for granted that the identity of the resurrected body with the earthly body is secured through the identity of the spiritual reality and not through the identity of secondary

[14] J. Ratzinger, "Auferstehungsleib," in *Lexikon für Theologie und Kirche* I, pp. 1052f.; J. Schmitt, "Auferstehung Christi," *ibid.*, pp. 1028-35, esp. p. 1031.—Insofar as the resurrected body implies authentic "bodiliness", it stands out in the glorified condition of the world which we call "heaven" and which is beyond our senses as they are now. To construct here something too heavily "visible" would lead, especially in the borderline experience of death, to greater difficulties in understanding than a somewhat spiritualizing approach. In this sense one can here apply Y. Congar's criticism of a "physical explanation of the last things": there is no such thing as a physical explanation of the resurrection.

[15] See footnote 13.

physical factors. But one is free to hold this on the ground of a broad theological tradition.[16] That we can also say with Romans, Ephesians, Hebrews and the creed that Jesus descended into the underworld follows from the position taken up by the Synod of Sens in 1140 against Abelard. But we must remember that the soul is not meant as a part of man, but rather as the human soul (as distinct from the Logos without a soul of the Apollinarians).

The soul was therefore in the underworld, not merely by some external action, some manifestation of power, but in its very "substance" (Denzinger, 385). The presence must therefore have been something more intensive than a mere action. But this example shows once again how necessary it is for modern theology to give more thought to such notions as "substance", "matter", "spirit" ("soul") and "body". For completeness' sake I may add that the patristic and Oriental tradition thinks in no other terms than those here put forward about the glorification of Christ before the earthly experience of the resurrection.

2. Before we reflect upon what Jesus achieved in the underworld, we have to ask ourselves what happened to him in the descent into hell. For our sake he underwent the death of a sinner (2 Cor. 5, 21; cf. 2 Pet. 2, 22), although he was wholly without sin (Heb. 4, 15). Until Christ and in Christ this death, however, meant the descent into the *sheol* (the Jewish underworld of the dead). What made death so intolerable for the Israelites, i.e., for the people who lived in Jesus' immediate environment, was not so much the cessation of life on earth with its happiness, or even the transference to a joyless, shadowy existence—which is the meaning of *sheol* [17]—but the conviction that death broke off all relationship with God (Is. 38, 11; Ps. 6, 6; 88, 6 and 8, and elsewhere).[18] Now, since Jesus himself in the anguish of death

---

[16] Evidence for this may be found in H. Vorgrimler, "Auferstehung des Fleisches," in *Lebendiges Zeugnis* (Paderborn, May, 1963), pp. 50-65, esp. pp. 60f.; J. Ratzinger, see above, footnote 14.

[17] H. Eising, "Scheol," in *Lexikon für Theologie und Kirche* IX, pp. 391-3.

[18] F. Dingemann, "Tod im Alten Testament," in *Lexikon für Theologie und Kirche* X, pp. 218f.

cried out that he was abandoned by God (Matt. 27, 46; Ps. 22, 2) and for our sake died, innocent, the death of a sinner, it is obvious that in death he descended into the underworld, i.e. the *sheol*. Jesus died our death, i.e., he himself experienced the *sheol*. According to the notion of death held by the Jews of the Old Testament, his descent into the underworld cannot be attributed to some "new" initiative, but it is rather implied in his very death.

Compared with the biblical concept of death it becomes clear that Calvin's interpretation is not tenable. In his *Institutions* (II, 16, 10f.) Calvin maintained that Jesus experienced "the dreadful torments of the damned and the lost in his soul" and took upon himself after his death through some new activity the real torments of the damned in hell. This is not true. He rather took upon himself the hidden and ambivalent experience of the sinner's death and so, through his death, found himself—one might almost say, naturally—in the situation of the *sheol*. But as we say "in his death", it is clear that the question of "how long?" is basically of no consequence. If Jesus has taken upon himself the situation of being reduced to utter powerlessness and of being abandoned by God, is there still a point in asking whether this lasted for about three full human days (of twenty-four hours!)? We should therefore say that wherever the death of Jesus is proclaimed as a truly human, hidden death full of its own ambiguities, we truly confess his descent into hell. In catechesis we should therefore not say: after his death Jesus decided "Let us go down into hell"; the decision to suffer man's descent into hell is rather contained in the decision Jesus took to die the death of man.

3. Only at this point do we meet what is new in the teaching about the descent, because it is precisely Jesus, and not an ordinary human being, who took upon himself the condition of the *sheol*. In suffering this wholly human death Jesus becomes "at one" with those who died this death before him. His death does not lead into solitude but into the community of mankind. This refers, first of all, not to the living human beings who are

leading a far from shadowy existence, but to the dead. It is to them that Jesus joins himself. Or to put it better, with H. Urs von Balthasar: his descent takes place not in the history which is actually happening, but in the history of what has happened.[19]

To see the full implications of this we must think ourselves into the situation and realize that these dead did not sleep the sleep of death. They were alive, without joy, without God. The question whether there was still any hope of fulfillment for these creatures, i.e. for that whole pitiable upshot of human history before Christ, must be seen against the background of the fact that heaven exists only through Jesus Christ.[20] Because of this fact, the unredeemed mass of mankind before Christ can rightly be described as "hell". And now it is not difficult to see what it means when Jesus, at least in his spiritual activity, does not only share man's life and death, but also that fate of past "deadness" which was implied in man's death. The conclusions which may be drawn even only from the dogma of the hypostatic union in relation to all this have been indicated by Karl Rahner in his theology of Holy Saturday.[21]

But Scripture mentions not only that Jesus (in his descent) shared in the human fatality of death, but it says explicitly that Christ's presence in the *sheol* was an active presence. It uses the term *kerygma* in 1 Peter 3, 19, and speaks of "leading out the captives" where it joins Ps. 68, 19, with the text of Eph. 4, 8 and 9. This activity of Christ in hell is a saving activity. It is interesting (and so far nobody seems to have noticed it) that in the Coptic and Ethiopic versions of the creed used after baptism the descent is described as a freeing of those who were shackled (*liberavit vinctos:* Denzinger-Schönmetzer 62, 63). This seems to be another proof that the "binding and loosing" has a deeper implication than these words usually are given.[22]

[19] *Op. cit.,* pp. 409f.
[20] J. Ratzinger, "Himmel," in *Lexikon für Theologie und Kirche* V, pp. 355-8.
[21] Cf. footnote 4.
[22] I have tried to point this out in various ways, and summarized it in my essay, "Matthieu 16, 18f. et le sacrement de pénitence: L'homme devant Dieu," in *Mélanges H. de Lubac* I (Paris, 1964), pp. 51-61.

And so the doctrine of Christ's descent into hell becomes a point which, in an exceptional way, expresses the implications of the redemption. And this is not adequately brought out in the biblical and dogmatic treatment of redemption.

III

THE DESCENT INTO HELL
AND THE UNIVERSALITY OF THE REDEMPTION

All this has further consequences for other sectors of dogmatic theology. To explain it we shall have to go a little deeper. If we take an average manual of dogmatic theology[23] we may read there, for instance: "Unfortunately, the sources of revelation do not help us in working out a topography of the beyond." At least an honest statement. This is all the more remarkable since the same author is greatly disturbed, shortly afterward, in his attempt to work out four different "camps" for those that don't belong: "hell as the place of the damned", the "fire of purgatory", the "lap of unbaptized infants" and the "lap of the forefathers". According to this learned author it is "impossible" that Christ descended into the hell of the damned; this would "lack any intelligible purpose" and would "contradict the divine dignity of the Son of God". He allows as a "pious opinion" that Christ at least consoled the poor souls in purgatory, but this opinion will hardly stand up to deeper reflection. That Christ appeared in the "lap of the unbaptized infants" is an opinion which "lacks any serious foundation". As the author says: "He can neither help these souls, nor can he triumph over them." So there remains the "lap of the forefathers" where "the old fathers and the just of the Old Testament waited to be admitted to the beatific vision after they would be purified from all stain of sin in purgatory". It strikes this learned dogmatic theologian as regrettable that, in connection with the descent of Christ, 1 Peter says nothing about the just of the Old Testament and explicitly lets the saving kerygma be addressed to those that were

[23] See, for example, the work cited in footnote 11, pp. 281-4.

disobedient at the time of Noah. Whether this concerned those that perished in the flood, i.e., particularly the godless, or the "sons of God" of Genesis 6, they were all "unjust".[24]

One of the first questions that concerns dogmatic theology is therefore that of the "limbo" and purgatory. Are these different places or different situations? If the answer is affirmative— and this holds, in my opinion, for both—why are the biblical texts about the descent explicitly concerned with the unjust? Why is there no mention of Abraham and Moses? And what is more according to the Scriptures: the construction of these four conditions (whether described as places or as situations), or von Balthasar's thesis according to which Christ stirred up the stagnation of the *sheol* and evacuated it, which led to the creation of purgatory as a purifying passage?[25] The second question will have to be whether man-made theories can be allowed to impose limits on Christ's redemption. According to this kind of bookish scholasticism nothing passes through hell, purgatory or limbo. Even in the "limbo" of the forefathers nothing much happened. Our author says: "Frankly speaking, the joyful message of Christ was limited to a preliminary announcement that they would be set free, because the formal admission to the place of the blessed took place only on Ascension day (Ps. 67, 19)." In other words, Christ went down to those who had been "imprisoned" for several thousand years and told them that they would be set free in "forty days". This kind of dogmatic scholasticism sees nothing more real in the descent of Christ—an example of unconscious comedy, as von Balthasar says. It is true that after death there is no more room for further decisions, for repentance or conversion. But what entitles this dogmatism to put limits on the sovereignty of God's grace? Has this system taken seriously enough what is said about the descent in 1 Peter 4, 6? "For this is why the gospel was preached even to the dead, that though judged in the flesh like men, they might live in the spirit like God."—To the dead, the unjust . . .

---

[24] K. Schelkle, *op. cit.*, pp. 105-7.
[25] *Op. cit.*, pp. 409f.

Perhaps I have managed to show that in a certain type of scholasticism human cleverness has done a great deal of damage to the universality of redemption, looked at retrospectively. If it is typical of a myth that it tries to hem in God's freedom by confining it to compulsory action, we may well ask how far such a theology, centered on sin, forces God into a system of guilty actions and of correspondingly obligatory reprisals by God, and so becomes itself a mythological creation.

For the moment I cannot wholly accept von Balthasar's thesis that Christ has freed us once and for all from hell,[26] in spite of the fact that he is supported by a strong tradition both in the East and the West. I would simply like to pose the question which arises from this doctrine of the descent of Christ: if the doctrine of the descent implies, retrospectively, a universality of redemption, and if scholasticism has failed to understand the full significance of this doctrine, what does this mean, prospectively, for our ecclesiology (e.g., in connection with the point in time when the Church was founded and with the phrase *extra Ecclesiam nulla salus* (there is no salvation outside the Church) and for our usual, static view of eschatology? Perhaps one cannot go so far as von Balthasar and say that "theology has forgotten God", but we certainly cannot maintain that enough respect was paid to God's grace and the mystery of it in every document of the magisterium.

As can be seen, the doctrine of Christ's descent into hell affects many dogmatic treatises; at the same time it is a significant point for the convergence of dogmatic and moral theology on the one hand, and for that of exegesis and dogma on the other. It should also have an important message for that badly neglected theology of mysticism, insofar as one would have to consider that in the imitation of Christ there is room for descents into hell of ordinary Christians, not spontaneously but in obedience to a divine mandate,[27] and this, in turn, opens up new perspectives for the pastoral approach.

[26] Hans Urs von Balthasar, *Die Gottesfrage des heutigen Menschen* (Vienna, 1956), pp. 187-204.
[27] *Ibid.*, pp. 194ff.

BIOGRAPHICAL NOTES

YVES CONGAR, O.P.: Born April 13, 1904, in Sedan, France. He became a Dominican, and was ordained in 1930. He pursued his philosophical studies at the Institut Catholique in Paris, and theology at Le Saulchoir in Etiolles, France. From 1931 to 1954 he was Professor of Fundamental Theology and Ecclesiology at Le Saulchoir. His published works are numerous and erudite. Among them are *Lay People in the Church* (1957), *After Nine Hundred Years* (1959), *Laity, Church and World* (1960), *The Mystery of the Church* (1960), *The Mystery of the Temple* (1962), and *The Meaning of Tradition* (1964).

JOSEPH BOURKE, O.P.: Born March 26, 1926, in Birmingham, England. He became a Dominican, and was ordained in 1954. He pursued his studies at the Angelicum, Rome, the Ecole Biblique in Jerusalem, and Oxford University, earning his doctorate at Oxford in 1965. During 1958 and 1959 he taught Sacred Scripture at Hawkesyard, and since then has lectured on Old Testament Exegesis at Blackfriars, Oxford. His published works include many contributions to scholarly journals such as *The Catholic Biblical Quarterly, Scripture, Life of the Spirit, Blackfriars,* and *Revue Biblique.*

PIET SCHOONENBERG, S.J.: Born October 1, 1911, in Amsterdam, the Netherlands. He became a Jesuit, and was ordained in 1939. He studied philosophy in Nijmegen, theology in Maastricht, and attended the Institut Biblique in Rome, earning his doctorate in dogmatic theology in 1948. He became Professor of Dogmatic Theology at Maastricht, and has been to the United States as Visiting Professor in Pittsburgh. His published works include *God's World in the Making,* and regular contributions to theological and catechetical journals.

JOSÉ MARÍA GONZÁLEZ-RUIZ: Born May 5, 1916, he was ordained in 1939 for the Diocese of Málaga, Spain. He studied at the Gregorian University and the Institut Biblique, both in Rome, earning his doctorate in theology in 1940 and the licentiate in Sacred Scripture in 1953. He taught Greek at the seminary in Seville, was pastor of a parish in Seville, and Professor of New Testament at the seminary in Málaga as well as at the University of Salamanca. His published works include a number of books on St. Paul, and numerous articles for biblical encyclopedias and journals.

161

ENGELBERT GUTWENGER, S.J.: Born June 6, 1905, in Essen, West Germany. He became a Jesuit, and was ordained in 1936. He pursued his philosophical studies in Munich, and theology in Innsbruck, earning doctorates in both fields. He is Professor of Dogmatic and Fundamental Theology, was Dean of the Theological Faculty at Innsbruck from 1959 to 1960, and Rector of the University of Innsbruck in 1961 and 1962. His published works include philosophical and theological books and articles, and contributions to theological reviews.

HELMUT RIEDLINGER: Born February 17, 1923, in Konstanz, W. Germany. He was ordained in 1951 for the Diocese of Freiburg in Breisgau. After studying at the University of Freiburg and at the Gregorian University in Rome, he earned his doctorate in theology in 1956. Since June, 1965, he has been Professor of Dogmatic Theology at the University of Freiburg. His published works include several books and contributions to theological reviews.

OLIVIER ROUSSEAU, O.S.B.: Born February 11, 1898, in Mons, Belgium. He became a Benedictine, and was ordained in 1922. He studied at the Benedictine Seminary at Louvain, and at the College of St. Anselm in Rome. He was Professor of Philosophy at Louvain from 1924 to 1930, Master of Novices at Amay and then at Chevetogne from 1930 to 1950, and since 1950 has been director of the journal *Irénikon*. His published works, both books and articles, run the range from patristic theology and the liturgy, to monastic and ecumenical studies.

HERBERT VORGRIMLER: Born January 4, 1929, in Freiburg im Breisgau, W. Germany, he was ordained in 1953. He pursued his philosophical and theological studies at Freiburg and Innsbruck. Since 1958 he has been an editor of the *Lexikon für Theologie und Kirche* in the areas of dogma, biblical and moral theology, and philosophy. He has edited commentaries on Vatican Council II, and directed the series *Quaestiones Disputatae*. Together with Karl Rahner, S.J., he has written the *Kleine Theologische Wörterbuch*, and is the author of an introduction to the life and work of Rahner which has been reprinted in six languages. In addition, he is the editor of several collections of essays.

EDWARD SCHILLEBEECKX, O.P.: Born in Antwerp, Belgium, November 12, 1914. He became a Dominican in 1934, and was ordained in 1941. He pursued his studies at Le Saulchoir in Etiolles, France and at the Sorbonne in Paris, becoming a master and doctor of theology. From 1943 to 1957 he taught at the Dominican Studium in Louvain, Belgium, and has been, since 1958, Professor of Dogmatic Theology at the University of Nijmegen, Holland. He is an advisor to the Dutch episcopacy at Vatican Council II. Among his many publications are: *The Sacramental Economy of Salvation* (1952); *Mary, Mother of the Redemption* (1964); *Christ, the Sacrament of the Encounter with God* (1963); *Huwelijk, aardse werkelijkheid en heilsmysterie*, Vol. I (1964).

BONIFACE WILLEMS, O.P.: Born in Rotterdam, Holland, December 4, 1926. He studied philosophy and theology with the Dominicans at Zwolle and Nijmegen, and was ordained in 1952. Further studies followed at the Universities of Münster, Basle and Straatsburg. He earned his doctorate in 1957 at Münster with the thesis, "Kirchenzugehörigkeit als Heilsnotwendigkeit." At present he is Professor of Dogmatic Theology at the Albertinum in Nijmegen. His theological interests are shown in many articles about the Church, as well as in his writings about such personalities as Karl Barth and Karl Jaspers: cf. his book *Karl Barth* (1963), and the collective work *Mens en God* (1963).

International Publishers of CONCILIUM

ENGLISH EDITION
Paulist Press
Glen Rock, N. J., U.S.A.

Burns & Oates Ltd.
25 Ashley Place
London, S.W.1

DUTCH EDITION
Uitgeverij Paul Brand, N. V.
Hilversum, Netherlands

FRENCH EDITION
Maison Mame ·
Tours/Paris, France

GERMAN EDITION
Verlagsanstalt Benziger & Co., A.G.
Einsiedeln, Switzerland

Matthias Grunewald-Verlag
Mainz, W. Germany

SPANISH EDITION
Ediciones Guadarrama
Madrid, Spain

PORTUGUESE EDITION
Livraria Morais Editora, Ltda.
Lisbon, Portugal

ITALIAN EDITION
Editrice Queriniana
Brescia, Italy